THE
EAST and WEST

The Christian Life East and West

Toward the Mutual Enrichment of Japanese and Western Christianity

James Houston

REGENT COLLEGE PUBLISHING
Vancouver, British Columbia

The Christian Life East and West
Copyright © 2017 James Houston

Regent College Publishing
5800 University Boulevard
Vancouver, BC V6T 2E4 Canada
www.regentpublishing.com

All rights reserved. No part of this publication may be reproduced, stored in a retrieval system, or transmitted, in any form or by any means, electronic, mechanical, photocopying, recording or otherwise, without the prior written permission of the author, except in the case of brief quotations embodied in critical articles and reviews.

Regent College Publishing is an imprint of the Regent Bookstore <www.regentbookstore.com>. Views expressed in works published by Regent College Publishing are those of the author and do not necessarily represent the official position of Regent College <www.regent-college.edu>.

ISBN 978-1-57383-534-3

Cataloguing in Publication information is available from Library and Archives Canada.

Cover artwork: "Gather 'Round" by Joy Banks

Contents

Foreword   1

1. Christian Identity in the Flux of Contemporary Globalization   6
2. Pragmatism, Institutionalism, and Technocracy Threaten Christianity, West or East   19
3. Family Relationships—Japanese, Western, and Christian   33
4. Personal Emotions—Classical, Japanese, Western, and Christian   49
5. Core Cultural Values of Relationship—Contexts of Friendship and Community, Japanese and Western   64
6. Maturity and Wisdom in the Seasons of Life   78
7. Enriched by Christian Japanese Insights on Suffering, Silence, and Beauty   90

Conclusion   105

Foreword

Globally, all Christians need to recognize that God has created all humanity in "his image and likeness," the *imago dei* (Gen. 1:21). It should not surprise us then that among all the religions, as well as with secularists and atheists, we find as our neighbors, good, kind, truthful, compassionate people, for as human beings—whether they know God or worship idols, or are skeptical of all religions—their human morality is God-given. It is God, as Creator, who has made humans to be religious beings.[1]

Cultural awareness of globalization began to be popularized with the study of comparative religions at the end of the nineteenth century, at a convention in Chicago. A Christian missional approach followed soon after in Edinburgh, Scotland in 1910, while the World Council of Churches has had a long discourse during the twentieth century. More recently, reports from Christian communities in regions of persecution or national distress has informed us of their affliction. New shapes to global missional policies, or predictive demographic studies of the reversal of Christian growth from the northern to the southern hemispheres, are dramatically occurring. In this fluidity of globalization, it becomes more important than ever to sustain one's own eth-

---

1. Even an elaborate religion like Buddhism echoes more of the Old Testament mythos of Genesis 1-3 than is commonly recognized, but always having a converse perspective: forest not garden; elephant not a willy serpent; animals fatefully controlling the destiny of humans, not humans as co-regents over the animal realm; and Nature replacing the Creator.

nicities as being expressive of each being a member within the body of Christ, for this diversity is what enriches us all.

The choice of a dialogue between Japanese and Western Christians is distinctive because of the history of Japan, over the past two centuries in particular, to imitate and readily embrace Western values. Christians should behave differently, upholding their own ethnicity, whatever it is, as being transformed by the Gospel. As I learnt to sing in the Sunday school 90 years ago:

> Jesus loves the little children,
> All the children in the world:
> Black and yellow, red and white,
> All are precious in his sight,
> Jesus loves all the children of the world!

Likewise, Christian Japanese women should not be tempted to become "westernized" to become sexually free, but should learn to become "free in Christ," to remain more richly Japanese women! Nor should Japanese male pastors be entrapped in the American cult of "leadership," which is foreign to Japanese culture.

The apostle Paul remained a Jew throughout his life, urging the Corinthian Christians, likewise, "to remain in your calling," within their ethnic identities.[2] Yet he was freed from Judaism, claiming that his freedom in Christ permitted him to be "a Jew to the Jews"—"to those under the law I became one as under the law," "to those outside the law I

---

2. J. Brian Tucker, *"Remain in your Calling": Paul and the Continuation of Social Identities in 1 Corinthians*, (Eugene, Oregon: Wipf & Stock, Pub.: 2011).

became as one outside the law," "yet never outside the law of God but under the law of Christ" (1 Cor. 9:19-23). The apostle lived out this "global flexibility" all for the sake of the Gospel of Christ. It is this Pauline freedom and mandate we wish to explore. Thereby, he learnt to be accepting and appreciative transculturally: "...whatever is true, whatever is honorable, whatever is pure, whatever is just, whatever is lovely, whatever is commendable, if there is anything worthy of praise, think about these things" (Phil. 4:8). This then is our mandate and freedom to imitate the apostle.

In the journey of life, we can distinguish between life viewed from the window, and life experienced on the road. I started to prepare these essays in my home in Canada, reading many books on Japanese culture, like viewing Japanese "from the window." But when I began with my wife and then my daughter to travel with Japanese friends in Japan, to experience deeper relationships with Japanese Christians, we experienced, in their fears, frustrations, and sufferings, a very different perspective. For we found, as human beings, we are all universally desirous of being freed from diverse sources of fear, with the same need of love, the same desire for friendships, which only God can give us. For all human beings are relational beings, ambiguously living between fear and love.

Within our diverse cultural heritages, we can express our humanity in many richly diverse ways. But only when we have changing perspectives, in the stages of our cultural or more personal lives, will we know that we are "travelling on the way of life"—not being static, as when we only "look from the window." Perhaps that is what we all need: changing perspectives every day, to indicate we are travelling, or living, by growing afresh.

Yet we need to be "pilgrims," not "tourists," as globalization is now facilitating. For a "tourist" is being merely curious, not involved and engaged with one another transculturally. Many Japanese girls love reading the novels of Anne of Green Gables. Even though they do not know that the origin of L.M. Montgomery's novels is "Christian," they perhaps sense Anne and her playmates had an inner freedom foreign to their own heritage. So Prince Edward Island is crowded every summer with these young Japanese tourists, keen to enter the house in which Anne actually lived. But it remains just that—the satisfaction of a tourist curiosity; their own lives are not changed. Just a very few may become Christians, who beyond their own natural curiosity are seeking to become that rare group of seekers, spiritual pilgrims.

Likewise, I do not as an author want to be merely a "tourist" in Japan. Recently, my daughter Claire and I set out to grow deeper in our faith in a visit to Japan. We were further building upon previous visits made with my wife, Rita, who loved her "Japanese daughters" who had lived with us each for a year or more in our family home in Vancouver. As their spiritual "mother," she inspired each to become relationally "free" from their Japanese heritage of sexual non-equality.

From this personal family encounter has grown this book, to encourage much more cross-cultural dialogue and friendships within global Christianity. It is only a tentative introduction, to explore what new insights Christian faith can take us through this remarkable twenty-first century. It is like "seeing Christianity again in a fresh way," as new prophets anticipate a new "global Christendom." As we have already emphasized, the choice of Japanese and Western cultures is deliberate, since perhaps Japan more than any other culture has embraced the Western culture, in sharp—even tragic—contrast to other major cultures of the world, now clashing with each other. Can Japanese and Western Christians mutually enable each other to critique the distortions we are always making of calling ourselves "Christians"? The following essays explore this quest.

They are a tentative reflection of what both Western and Japanese Christians may be guided to appreciate in each other so distinctively and to learn from each other's culture. For we find, as in a dialogue between reader and author, that the excesses in either culture actually distort the Gospel of Christ, and both separate us unnecessarily. For example, the intensity of "social belonging" in the *amae* of Japanese culture and the exaggerated individualism of Western culture both distort Biblical faith and practice.[3] Yet each in moderation can enrich the other, when accepted in a truly Christian spirit. May then the Holy Spirit guide and inspire us all, readers and author, in this common life "in Christ."

---

3. Actually, the Japanese are far better and more objective anthropologists than Westerns are about their own distinctive cultures, for the West has the *hubris* of being colonial nations trading with Japan in centuries past.

I

Christian Identity in the Flux of Contemporary Globalisation

Japan is ideally representative of contemporary globalization for a number of reasons. Firstly, because the common view that Japan is a mono-cultural and a mono-ethnic society is being challenged, whether applied to ancient or to modern times. The religious census will double or even triple the national statistics, because it is common for a Japanese to identify having two or even three religious identities—Buddhist, Shinto, "Christian." In the West it is more definitive whether one has a religious identity or not, although the strongest identifier has been that of the Boomer generation claiming a "professional identity." Becoming secularized and "Western" has followed this trend everywhere.

This confuses East Asian Christians into thinking that to take Christian faith more seriously one has to leave a secular profession, to enter into "pastoral ministry within the church." Actually, this is more Buddhist than Christian, as "wearing the saffron robe" suggests that a seriously committed Buddhist is one who will become a monk. But sustaining a strong "Christian" identity—for all professional sources of social identity, in all callings of life—is a great challenge, West or East.

Geography and History Shape All Cultures

Japan is peculiarly favored to sustain a strong identity in resisting the fluidity of modern globalization. Europe has always been fragmented by its diverse environments and historic changes. China has been remarkable in its continental scale. This has tended to create a much more inward-looking series of cultures even though China has had intense diversification on its western frontiers. But overall its worldview of heaven has been universal. Indeed, China has the longest historical continuity of any global culture. It began trading across the Indian Ocean in the time of the Egyptian Pharaohs!

But as a society of islands, separated from Asia by dangerous seas, Japan was able to develop in relative isolation, while its mountainous backbone restricted the habitable land for a congested society. This forced its people to live in social harmony, which is what the word *wa* means. Its peasant farmers also had to co-operate, as rice-farming, which needed strong co-operative help, became its main food supply after 300 A.D. Thus, group objectives were strengthened, to create a culture of *amae*, or social belonging. However, this internalized the basic emotion of fear, as "social fear" developed against saying anything that might penalize complaint with social ostracism, or *murahachibu*.

Global Threats to Our Humanity in the Twentieth Century

But the fluidity of Western culture has been almost apocalyptic in contrast during the nightmarish twentieth century, with its militarism and ideologies.

Two great cities of Japan were wiped out in nuclear attacks. The holocaust was an attempted genocide of the Jews by the demonic romanticism of the Nazis. The fantasy of communism slaughtered even more millions, while two world wars contributed to further genocides of our youth. The Romanian dictator even tried to generate a new human species of "Socialist Man," experimenting with untold hundreds of thousands of small children.

Christendom seemed asleep to these outrages apart from a few brave prophetic voices. One was the Swiss theologian Karl Barth, the first to speak of "theo-anthropology," as the unique Christian identity. Famously, Barth declared: "The nature of the man Jesus, alone is the key to the problem of human nature."[1] He was aware of some of these terrifying experiments to re-create humanity. While Barth was opposing the Nazification of the German National Lutheran Church, another courageous prophetic voice was that of Cardinal Wojtyla, later Pope John Paul II, in Poland,

---

1. Karl Barth, *Church Dogmatics* (London: T.& T. Clark, 2004), vol. III/2, p. 193.

standing against the notion of "Socialist Man."[2] Both were engaged in the prophetic recovery of all humanity, as being created in "the image and likeness of God," or the *imago dei*.

Now, more insidiously, further threat to the nature of being human has arisen globally since World War II in being identified with "Secularist Man." This time it has been ironically Islamic militants, not Christians, who have, with gunfire since their first attack of 9/11 (2001), communicated to the world that man is still a religious being. For Christians, this tragic world turmoil is challenging us afresh to re-interpret "theo-anthropology," with greater urgency than ever. For the new age of quantum computers will in the next few years outpace human intelligence with artificial intelligence. Only closer cross-cultural unity among all Christians will deepen and more deeply enrich our common humanity. Our Christian global future lies in becoming "more genuine human beings," by the grace of our Creator.

The First Global Curiosity over Ethnic Differences

Perhaps the last time Christians were engaged in such a global comparison of what it means to be "human" was in the early sixteenth century, when the Spaniards "discovered" what was to them a new continent, "the Americas." Soon after Columbus' discovery, a Catholic commission was sent out to the Greater Antilles Islands, to assess whether the natives had "a soul," or were just a strange new species of animal. Meanwhile, the natives were busy drowning their strange

2. John Paul II, *Man and Woman He Created Them: A Theology of the Body,* trans. Michael Waldstein (Boston: Pauline Books & Media, 2006).

prisoners, to see if their "bodies" would decompose![3] The Spanish origins of comparative ethnology in the Americas then became a complex story.[4] Later European travelers, traversing the Americas, and coming upon so many ethnic groups, imagined themselves back in the Garden of Eden, now with a second mandate. Not only were they to "name the animals"—a great zoological task in itself, when a jaguar was not a lion, and there was a whole menagerie of other strange creatures to identify and classify—but now Christian travelers were given the further mandate to "name" all sorts of human beings they had never seen before, or known had ever existed except in phantasy.[5]

In this passing generation, Westerns assumed "the social sciences" had taught us all we need to know about our humanity, family, and social systems, etc. Instead, we are just beginning to learn that India, with yoga, and China, with breath techniques, are thousands of years ahead of the West in certain bodily skills. The visceral control of the Maoris is unsurpassed, for it was developed by spending hundreds of years sailing in primitive boats across the Pacific. The so-called primitive Aborigines of Australia have far more complex systems of marriage, inter-marriage, and family social

---

3. Claude Lévi-Strauss, *Race and History* (Paris: UNESCO, 1952), p. 12.

4. Anthony Pagden, *The Fall of Natural Man: The American Indian and the Origins of Comparative Ethnology* (Cambridge: Cambridge University Press, 1982).

5. Gordon M. Sayre, *Les Sauvages Americains: Representations of Native Americans in French and English Colonial Literature* (Chapel Hill/London: The University of North Carolina Press, 1997).

life than we can yet imagine.[6] Western parents have a lot to learn from the initiation ceremonies of youth, in the role played by music, as exercised by the primitive tribes of the Venda, in the remote northern mountains of South Africa.[7] All of us can anticipate a renewed experience of being human in a robotic age the more we learn from our ancestors.

Responding Christianly to Global Ethnicity Today

Analogously, can we anticipate Christianity will be further enriched in new ways in this twenty-first century? I believe we can. Christians have been themselves divided into the three great groups—of Roman Catholic, various Eastern Orthodox groups, and Protestant. Now they are beginning to enter more into dialogue, and less into isolated proclamations, than ever before. Within our Protestant denominations, we, too, are questioning previous sources of church identity and their emphases upon particular "doctrines." Young people today are much more indifferent to these historical legacies, as they are forming more spontaneously their own friendship groups. Church leaderships are becom-

---

6. Claude Lévi-Strauss, *Race and History, op. cit.,* pp. 27-28.
7. John Blacking, *How Musical is Man?* (Seattle/London: University of Washington Press, 1974).

ing more de-professionalized, as "the priesthood of all believers" becomes exercised more spontaneously.

Remaining in Our Ethnic Calling

Reflecting upon the turbulence and rapidity of cultural and societal changes today, we could feel very unstable. These essays may seem to make it worse for our fluid identities. We have already cited the example of the apostle Paul, but we can elaborate this further. He was a Jew, originally a very radical Jew, who set out on a crusade to reform Judaism, as a "Pharisee of the Pharisees." Then, he began purging the Christians who seemed to be destroying all forms of Judaism and were an even worse threat! Before Saul of Tarsus was converted on the Damascus road, he was aggressively active within Judaism itself as a "double reformer."

First of all, he was seeking to reform Jerusalem Judaism, having spent his boyhood on the fringe of strict Judaism, in Tarsus, to the north of Palestine. He had come to be further educated in Jerusalem—suggesting his parents were well-to-do—probably first learning Greek script, and then learning Hebrew script, together with Aramaic, the oral language of Palestine. Even though he was born in Tarsus, the metropolis of Cilicia in Syria (Acts 21:39;22:3), he came from a devout Jewish family that belonged to the Pharisaic reformed movement. He traced his lineage to the tribe of Benjamin, and was brought up by his parents to speak both Hebrew and Aramaic (Phil. 3:3; Gal. 1:14). His Hebrew name was Saul, or *Sa'ul,* and his Greek or Roman name *Paulos*, as he had Roman citizenship. His education was later to stand him in good stead on his missionary journeys, having contact with

Sergius Paulus, governor of Crete (Acts 13:4-12), and with later Asiarchs in Ephesus. With his childhood in Cilicia, he may have also known the native Cilician language also. In Jerusalem under the Rabbi Gamaliel, Paul studied the *Torah* from a Pharisaic perspective and also learned in a rhetorical school his later use of skillful persuasion.[8] Truly his claim was true: he was, indeed, a "Pharisee of the Pharisees."

Why did he then persecute the Christians? Jews like himself, who rejected the claims of other Jewish believers in Jesus, were convinced that faith in Jesus as the Messiah, and in the atoning efficacy of his death on the cross, was an attack on the foundations of Torah obedience as the basis of Israel's salvation, which Yahweh had revealed to Israel. First arresting Christians in Jerusalem, he then traveled to the old Syrian capital, Damascus, to arrest more of this dangerous "sect." But on his way he had a personal encounter with Jesus, "seeing the Lord" (1 Cor. 9:1), as an "appearance of the risen Christ" (1 Cor. 15: 8), to which Luke adds, "a light from heaven" (Acts 9:3; 22:6), indeed, "a great light above the brightness of the mid-day sun"(Acts 26:13). Falling down in recognition of Jesus, he heard him speak to him as Jesus Lord in heaven, exalted at the right hand of God. Later, welcomed by a Christian believer in Damascus, Ananias, Paul was informed that Jesus had commissioned him to proclaim his name to all the world, that is, Ananias

---

8. Eckhard J. Schnabel, *Paul the Missionary: Realities, Strategies and Methods* (Downers Grove, IL: IVP Academic, 2008), pp. 43-44.

too had heard Jesus speak to him personally (Acts 9:15-16; 22:14-15).[9]

What should also encourage us all, in our ethnic diversity today, is that the portrayal of Jesus was told and re-told in diverse ways by diverse witnesses, before the Gospels were written. As Paul states it, it could variously be described as "the Gospel for the circumcised" and "the Gospel for the uncircumcised" (Gal. 2:7). Its different out-workings caused tensions between Paul, Peter, and James.[10] The narratives and portraiture of Jesus remain different in the three first Gospels, while John's Gospel stands by itself, a unique presentation. All this encourages us, still today, to continue sharing our testimonies, our conversions, and our understandings of ethnic diversities.

But German scholar A. von Harnack, at the beginning of the twentieth century, interprets the apostle Paul as doing a terrible injustice to Judaism, "almost unprecedented in the annals of history." He claims:

> The Gentile Church stripped it of everything: she took away its sacred book; herself but a transformation of Judaism, she cut off all connection with the parent religion...By their rejection of Jesus, the Jewish people disowned their calling and dealt the death blow to their own existence... the place of the Jews was taken by the Christians as the new people, who appropriated the whole tradition of Judaism... Christians established

---

9. Ibid, p. 45.
10. James D.G. Dunn, *Neither Jew nor Greek, a Contested Identity* (Grand Rapids: Wm. B. Eerdmans, 2015), pp. 802-4.

themselves in the strongholds hitherto occupied by Jewish propaganda and Jewish proselytes.[11]

Little did the liberal scholar von Harnack realize that such violent rhetoric was to be used conversely by anti-Semitism in Germany, later in the twentieth century, by the attempt of the Nazis to wipe out the Jewish race in the Holocaust.

Instead, scholars today are taking a very different interpretation, the more they probe into the diversity of both the canonical witnesses of the New Testament scriptures, as well as the apocryphal sources of other "Gospels," such as *Thomas*. As the magisterial study of James Dunn concludes:

> ...the neglect of the Jewishness of Jesus has meant that the other great originating and definitive force in earliest Christianity, Paul, was less fully appreciated than he had been by the first Christian generations. For only when it is fully appreciated just how Jewish the first disciples of Jesus were, and how emerging Christianity was most straight-forwardly identified as a messianic sect of Judaism, only then can the contribution of Paul be properly recognized. For it was Paul, in his insistence that the grace of God was free to all who believed, who ensured that the identity of Christianity would expand to include Gentile as well as Jew—and who ensured

---

11. A. von Harnack, *The Mission and Expansion of Christianity in the First Three Centuries* (London: E.T. Williams & Northgate, 1904-5), pp. 81, 82-3.

that the reconciliation between races and classes has to be seen as an inescapable part of the Gospel too.[12]

"In Christ" the Apostle Paul Protects All Our Ethnic Identities

In defense of the apostle Paul, we vigorously deny Harnack's veiled anti-Semitism, in his argument that the Apostle was destroying the Jewish identity in his Christian evangelism. Paul protects all of our diverse ethnic identities, while calling for a new source of identity as being found "in Christ." For he recognized that our "identity" lies at differing levels of social recognition. In the early church, there were some rich women subsidizing a local house-church, but there were also very poor, yet highly educated Greek slaves, business leaders, even members of the Imperial household. Yet they were all bonded as being "in Christ." Diverse ethnicity was a mark of the churches in Imperial Rome, or in a wealthy cosmopolitan city like Corinth, very different from the strongly Jewish peasant poverty of Christians in Palestine.

In writing his first pastoral epistle to the Corinthian Christians, the apostle writes with a strong conviction of "his own calling" to change the social identities of these diverse social groups as seen through Roman eyes to identities now being transformed into the image and likeness of Christ. He is now urging a "new unity" among them, when naturally they could so easily be divided. In 1 Corinthians 7: 17-24, he is not calling on them to seek social mobility, and change their status before their fellow citizens of Corinth. To be circumcised was the physical mark that one was an

---

12. James D. G. Dunn, *Neither Jew nor Greek, op. cit.* pp. 823-4.

ethical Jew, while its absence was that one was birthed in a pagan household. These were now previous sources of identity, like observing physical facial differences, whereas being "in Christ" is a wholly different relational distinction.

At the close of the first century A.D., the early Christian text of 1 Clement (c.93-97) opens with a greeting from one group of alien Christians to another: "The church of God residing as aliens (*paroikousa*) in Rome to the church of God residing as aliens (*paroikouse*) in Corinth." Later Polycarp was to write his *Letter to the Philippians* (c. 117-120), then considered an alien church. As Hebrews 11:23 put it eloquently: "they confessed that they were strangers and sojourners on the earth." Paul himself had written to the Philippian church that they were "looking for a heavenly citizenship" (Phil. 3:20). This eschatological perspective was drawn from beyond the circumstances of the Roman empire—it originated in the Hebrew Bible, with "Exodus and Exile" being the *leit-motif* of Israelite identity.

Yet, as Martin Hengel has observed, it was precisely this early Christian alienation that gave such small groups of Christians a new freedom, a new power, to overcome all the oppression and insults of the next three centuries, from the Roman state authorities. It was what Paul himself had experienced as salvation—a strong inner detachment from such fears, which allowed him to assure his fellow Christians that "our citizenship is in heaven" (Phil. 3:20).

However, it is the cognitive bias of scholarship to discover, explore, and focus upon one aspect of the truth. Again, what actually happened to the early Christians was *some* were persecuted, *some* felt being alien, *some* were martyred. But *others* lived very different lives—yet again *all* could claim to be "in Christ." Such is the power of "the name of Jesus Christ," for all our identities. In the sight of God, we are *all* nevertheless united "in Christ."

2

Pragmatism, Institutionalism, and Technocracy Threaten Christianity, East or West

Navigating between the possible and the impossible has always engendered the Japanese to develop their own type of pragmatism. For typhoons, floods, frequent earthquakes, as well as constant warfare among its warlords, have wrought constant suffering. All these have been borne stoically without complaint, as the negativity of the Buddhist world-view reinforced this as being a meaningless, fatalistic—and therefore unexamined—emotion. This, too, is a kind of pragmatism, which we will explore more deeply.

Institutionalism Is Pragmatic

A dictionary will define an institution as "an organization deemed appropriate for the purpose it is created to fulfil." Being "pragmatic" is defined as being practical, busy, perhaps officious and dogmatic, as well. World-wide, professional identities in urban life are more consistently pragmatic and stable than the fluidity of a religious identity. But the more "official" or "national" religions are, the more they, too, are "pragmatic."

Yet denominational affiliation does not really define true Christian identity, West or East. For example, the Anglican church of England was first framed by Queen Elizabeth, within her foreign policy of "balance of power," as she fought to divide France from Spain, in her pragmatic diplomacy. To this day, the Anglican church has been divided between the Anglo-Catholic party, originally for pro-Catholic Spain, from the Dutch Calvinists or "low party" of later Puritanism. The "via media" between them has eventually destroyed Anglican unity by its increasing liberalism. Such ecclesiastical history is endless.

It is basic to our human limitations that we all need to be "practical" rather than wholly "idealistic." But the more people are involved, the more social adjustments we need to make to accommodate everyone. This is true whether we are relating to a secular organization, such as a business, or a political state—large or small—as well as a denomination, or a church community. From the outside, Westerns may accuse the Japanese of being "more socially pragmatic," because their culture is more social in its identity, whereas Western cultures are more individualistic and less accommodating to "everyone." But from a Biblical view "all have sinned and come short of the glory of God" (Rom. 3:23), that is, all do not have an appropriate relationship with God, which is that of Biblical righteousness.

From a Christian standpoint, the central issue is: how sacrificial is our life, personal and corporate, in calling ourselves "Christian"? For, "being a Christian" we can make no compromises to the moral lassitude of non-Christians, even though both may be outwardly judged as "good people." Likewise, our differing cultural histories will reveal periods when the whole cultural community was more or less "pragmatic," reflecting when it was more acceptable or more persecuted as witnesses of Christ. Since each society has had its own distinctive history, the historical as well as cultural perspectives are both needed. That is why we are mutually inspired and enriched by learning globally, as well as historically, what it has meant to be "a Christian," or "a Christian community," in all our diversities, through diverse periods of the past.

The Fragmentation of Past Histories

As never before, mass migrations of ethnic groups are challenging all our cultures, East and West, North and South. For the first time, we are learning much more of the remarkable diversities of human beings. In my own city of Vancouver, Syrian migrants are now being welcomed by Christian communities. Yet the Christian hosts remain suspicious of how "orthodox" their adherents to the Assyrian Church may be! Canadian Christians are not aware, without knowledge of church history, that at the Council of Chalcedon in 485 A.D. the Assyrian Christians actually separated from the Western churches over Western speculation about how Christ was both human and divine. Was he the divine Son of God by his miracles, and human by the teaching of his parables? No, rebutted the Assyrian Christians, we hold in tension the mystery of his Incarnation, not to speculate doctrinally what is "human" and what is "divine" about the Son of God. Yet, early Western Christians then persecuted and made martyrs of Assyrian Christians, in the name of orthodoxy, not realizing they were less orthodox than their Assyrian brethren!

At even a personal level, I have lived to see my own students persecuted for their deeper knowledge of church history than their "Christian persecutors." One student was expelled from his denomination for exposing the false doctrine upon which that denomination was founded, even though its leaders today simply choose to ignore this heritage. Another student was nearly failed by his external examiner for his doctoral thesis, for exposing more than one original source of "Puritanism," which is both Calvinist and Ignatian! Others we know, whose standard of intellect were certainly worthy of high acceptance, were nearly failed by so-called "open-minded" secular examiners for being "narrow-minded" as Christians. One remarkable friend, who made a brilliant contribution to the Septuagint period of church history, spent 25 years in legal action against the rejection of her work, before a world-renowned university finally admitted that her case had been just. Her secular examiner had been a proud, secular bigot.

We are not advocating that all Christians need to have such "depth" of understanding regarding the origins and growth of Christianity. But all Christians should know that "truth is history." For God entered into history when God created human beings, and it is expressive of our humanity to be historical agents under God, who has acted historically. Now globally today, with far greater intermixture of ethnic diversity, we need deeper and richer history than ever before. A common knowledge of each other is what is required in our mutual acceptance of the "other." Yet "the digitalized culture" we are entering denies the relevance of the past, so that "history" is being overlooked for several reasons.

Pragmatism as "The Death of the Past"

What the Cambridge historian J.H. Plumb called "the death of the past," at the beginning of the Technological Revolution, in the late 1960's implied the "death of God."[1] This was the secular elimination of the religious history of the West. It was advocacy for the loss of transcendence, interpreting history as merely cause-and-effect imminence. It was the attempt to generate a new historiography—of a social history without God.

A second cause for "the loss of the past" is the youthful pre-occupation with one's own history, of messing around with a smart phone and with social media. It is all about "data-processing," which expands illusionary horizons of knowledge that now becomes a substitute for "wisdom." This is very dangerous for moral beings, who only live wisely when they use knowledge to have a sustainable moral life with other people.

A third cause for "the death of the past," is the orientation of "futurism," an obsession with looking forward instead of reviewing things historically, which has been seen in the aftermath of each creative revolution. In modern history, the first revolution was associated with the Renaissance, when human dreams were stimulated by "utopia"—literally *a tropos,* or "no place"—not placed on earth in time and space but only within one's creative imagination. Another

1. J. H. Plumb, *The Death of the Past* (New York: Columbia University Press, 1969).

arose after the harnessing of coal-steam-energy-communication of the Industrial Revolutions, each great country re-generated one after the other. Science fiction stimulated and popularized such futurism further, with star "wars" and "treks," and the increasing fascination with spaceships and dreams of planetary colonies.

Even serious science today is being harnessed by futurist thinking, in ignoring global stewardship of our habitable planet. Can the human rebellion against God intensify even further? Or should we begin to protest against yet another new tyranny, "the tyranny of secular scientists"? Not as a Christian, but as a humane philosopher, Paul Feyerabend has warned that objectivity and abstraction come to us at a very high price.[2]

In a further disturbing book, *From Human to Posthuman* (2006), another contemporary writer, Brent Waters, writes that the only thing standing in the way of the radical transformation of "nature," including human nature, is inadequate technology. He describes the cybernetic outlook as "only patterns or lines of information that can be erased and redrawn; no real limit that cannot be eventually overcome."[3] Since Japanese culture is enveloped in Nature,

---

2. Paul Feyerabend, *The Tyranny of Science* (Cambridge, U.K.: Polity Press, 2011).
3. Brent Waters, *From Human to Posthuman: Christian Theology and Technology in a Postmodern World* (Aldershot, U.K.: Ashgate Science & Religion series, ed. Roger Trigg & J. Wenstead van Huyssteen, 2006), p. x.

as the supreme god of the cosmos, it has no defense against "post-human" proposals, such as these cited by Waters.

For abstracting from subjective human experience tends to engender a new tyranny no different from the first great heresy of early Christianity, "Gnosticism." Futurism, in all its forms, is not innocent dreaming. It is the most dangerous of Christian heresies—Gnosticism wrapped up in new guise. The early Fathers saw this as the heresy above all other heresies, in denying the embodiment of Christian faith, in the advent of Jesus as the Son of God. For Christ became "flesh" to dwell among us. Abstraction denies this and ends up destroying our humanity.

However, the early Fathers were wise not to use the term "Gnosticism" as a generic category of heresy, but to speak only of individual "gnostics," challenging their variant false teachings. Irenaeus (c. 180 CE.) was the first to write an extensive attack, identifying the figure of Simon Magnus, who started as a Christian follower but, by attempting to buy the authority of the gift of the Holy Spirit (pragmatically we may say), ended up as an arch-enemy of the faith, and was revered by his followers in Rome as a god![4] Recognizing the same tendency in other heretics, Irenaeus could then group them all into the same genealogy as "gnostics," quarrelling among themselves over their various egotistical claims.

Tragically, I have had a "gnostic encounter" with one of my students. He came to me with the choice he had: either to teach in a small seminary in Asia with a few students, or to use his powers of "slaying with the spirit" to appeal to

---

4. Antti Marjanen, "Gnosticism" in *The Oxford University Handbook of Early Christian Studies,* ed. Susan Ashbrook Harvey and David C. Hunter (Oxford: Oxford University Press, 2008), p. 204.

thousands of followers. Pragmatically his seduction was to have this massive appeal, with godlike powers. Scholars may debate if "gnosticism" is past; no, its ramifications are vast into the future.

Responding Christianly to Technocracy

It is obvious Christians must think deeply into our cultures and their societies to respond appropriately.

1. First then, what is "culture"?

It originates in biological growth as a living cell, or as an agricultural category, separating wasteland from what has humanly been transformed, as a garden might be in a forest. It is then a reference to a higher state of human civilization. T.S. Eliot once observed there were three senses to a culture. "The first is that it has had a long historical source, and "no culture has appeared or developed without a religion… the culture will appear to be the product of the religion, or the religion the product of the culture."[5] The second is that a culture is analyzable as a geographic and historical entity, anthropological in focus, as we are focusing in this series of essays. The third is the balance of unity and diversity in religion—that is, universality with particularity of cult and devotion.[6]

But what the revolution of technocracy is doing is destroying all human cultures, to generate a global homogene-

---

5. T.S. Eliot, "Notes Towards the Definition of Culture," in *Christianity and Culture* (Santiago/New York: Harcourt Inc. 1948), p. 87.

6. Ibid, p. 88.

ity of the human race. As the philosopher Albert Borgmann has argued, when machine intelligence generates limitless data and experiences, with no boundaries, there will be no past or future, no particularity and diversity, indeed no differing human cultures.[7]

2. *What is technocracy?*

The ultimate contemporary shaping of pragmatism is what Jacques Ellul has called "la Technique."[8] Every time we ask "what technique can and should we use?" we are dimly aware how the technological mindset has become the most globally persuasive in the history of humanity, acting as a new "atmosphere" we are breathing every way, all the time. But we do not realize, as Ellul states: "Technique advocates the entire re-making of life and its framework,"[9] to remove physicality, to replace space and time, and to generate robots in place of human persons. All cultures are susceptible to this global invasion of "technique," but Japanese culture has its own susceptibility to its impersonal embrace, when the category of "Nature" has been so long absorbent of its culture. This leads us then to ask a third question.

3. *What does it mean to be a christian presence in our society?*

According to Jacques Ellul, just as Jesus prayed his disciples should be "*in* the world, but not *of* the world" (Jn. 17:

---

7. Albert Borgmann, "Pointless Perfection and Blessed Burdens," *Crux*, 47.4 (2011), pp. 20-8.

8. Jacques Ellul, *The Technological Society*, trans. By John Wilkinson (New York: Vintage, 1964).

9. Ibid, pp. 142-3.

11,14,16), Christians are here to witness to the grace and freedom of the Gospel. That is how they are a "presence" in the world.[10] Likewise, Paul Ricoeur has argued more implicitly in his book, *The Self as Another*, that our human identity is both "I" and "the Self for the Other."[11] Thereby we distinguish "the individual" from "the person." But technocracy would blur or eliminate the human agency, to replace it with a machine, regardless of race or culture. It would also obliterate the need of being human at all, if one machine can operate another machine *ad infinitum*. Yet even if quantum computers outpace and over-comprehend beyond the limits of human intelligence, they still need human beings to invent them and to use them. Human presence is needed to remain in a human world.

But the quality of that "human presence" is far greater if one is not acting egotistically, but more kindly and compassionately, as being "a self-for-the other." Then one becomes more of "a person," and less of "an individual." But being a "Christian" presence is incomparably more, if the agent is deeply dwelling daily in the presence of God, for then there is a deepening awareness that His Holy Spirit is more "present" than that of the human agent. Jean Vanier has exemplified this in being "present" to the mentally handicapped for whom only love can communicate. This love is

---

10. Jacques Ellul, *The Presence of the Kingdom,* 2nd ed. (Colorado Springs: Helmers & Howard, 1989), p. 19.

11. Paul Ricoeur, *The Self as the Other* (Chicago: The Chicago University Press, 1996).

for no other reason than to recognize the uniqueness of each member of the community that is sheltering them all.

Such "Christian presence" is unrestricted culturally, in time and space. It emancipates the emotional life, it transforms relationships, it deepens one's humanity, and extends one's horizons. Being a Christian is truly having a supernatural identity, yet one that is more human than any other source. It is revealed further by being expressive of deepest humility, while expressing its uniqueness. For the worship of the God and Father, through our Lord Jesus Christ, by the presence of the Holy Spirit, communicates the humility of God. For God became human that we should become godly. Profoundly then, does our robotic culture require a "Christian" presence.

4. How not to be secularised

The philosopher Charles Taylor has done a great service by helping us become free from the "malaise of the modern," indeed from "the brass heaven of immanence," or "the disenchantment with the secular."[12] Our concern is to co-ordinate cross-culturally, to understand how cultures other than the Western can also co-operate in the recovery of transcendence and of living before God in the world he has created with all its inhabitants.

As Taylor shows we need a long historical narrative, beyond the history of the machine-ages.[13] We need to be aware of the limitations of imminence, sensing the emp-

12. Charles Taylor, *The Malaise of the Modern* (Toronto: House of Ananasi Press, 2003).
13. Charles Taylor, *A Secular Age* (Cambridge, Mass.: Harvard University Press, Bellnap Press, 2007).

tiness and void of just being secularist, or even atheist. We need to recognize that simple truths such as 2×2=4, are unilateral in communication, but "deep truths," such that God exists, are bi-lateral communication that require metaphorical or symbolic language. It requires all forms of human communication, verbal or musical, gesture or silence. All genres are necessary—parable and folk-saying, mythology, narrative, story, laws, prophecy, psalmody, hymnody, discourse, letters, journals, rhetoric, or all the later forms of scholarly communication. All forms of reductionism must be recognized, then, as C.S. Lewis saw so clearly in his simple three lectures, on *The Abolition of Man*.[14]

5. What does it mean to be a personal agent of change in our society?

But as a Christian, Charles Taylor recognized we all need the experience of *metanoia*, a shattering of all our previous conceptions or world-views, to be enabled to make a paradigm shift from all our inherited past. Even Christians themselves may not be aware of how secular attitudes and habits have shaped and influenced them, and may be unable to critique the *zeitgeist*, or "spirit of the age," around them. Reform or a *conversion* as "a change around" are not enough. All of us need a change of identity.

The first new awareness is that each human being is unique before God, and uniqueness is his gift of grace to every human being. This alone shatters the technocratic/robotic mind-set. As a gift, this cannot be self-attained or

---

14. C.S. Lewis, *The Abolition of Man* (London: Faber & Faber, 1943).

induced, or perceived naturally, but can only be divinely inspired and received.

The second awareness is that creation is *complete*, so we now speak of it as "the created order."[15] This delineates an order of space and time, matter and spirit, which we explore intelligently in the diverse disciplines of the sciences. It becomes a comprehensible universe of the human mind—what Einstein called the greatest mystery of the cosmos. This sets us all "in place," learning to be "at home," not lost "in space." It also sets us "in time," as historical agents, serving our generation. As Qoheleth observed: "There is a time for everything, and a season for every activity under the heavens" (Eccl. 3:1). This provides and shapes human beings with a creaturely existence. Thus we can compare and be mutually enriched by what is Japanese and what is Western.

Yet uniqueness and unsubstitutability can be heavy burdens to bear. Does it mean I shall always be unbearably alone, never deeply recognized? Does it mean I carry response-abilities I cannot sustain? This is what Søren Kierkegaard called "despair,"[16] or what theologically we call "sin." The essence then of the modern secular spirit is to mortgage one's inheritance, acting like the Prodigal son, living riotously and irresponsibly in "the far country," fleeing from "space and time," and feeding at the pig-trough.

---

15. Oliver O'Donovan, *Resurrection and Moral Order: An Outline for Evangelical Ethics* (Grand Rapids: Wm. B. Eerdmans, 1986), p. 60.

16. Søren Kierkegaard, *The Sickness unto Death: A Psychological Exposition for Upbuilding and Awakening*, trans. By Howard V.& Edna H. Hong (Princeton: Princeton University Press, 1980), pp. 33-4.

As "the lost son," or the "lost humanity" today, perhaps we need to make "new connections."

3

Family Relationships—Japanese, Western, and Christian

Our first chapter outlined the threats we face from the de-personalizing forces of advanced technology. We are the most educated and intelligent human beings in our history. Yet it is ironic how our society has come to adopt animal pets, and to be fascinated by the animal origins of human ancestry. No longer are secularists quite sure how humans differ from animals in behaving as social/moral beings: in communication with each other; in the relations males and females have with each other; and in the degrees of bonding a baby animal has with its mother. But for Christians, being human has a supernatural basis, which Biblically is spelled out as "being created in the image and likeness of God" (Gen. 1:27). It is this which alone explains why human beings are so intrinsically relational. It is "the order of creation" that sets boundaries.

Popular interest in animals today, as being companionable as household pets, is especially appreciated by small children. But "it is a great puzzle," notes the anthropologist Rodney Needham, "that people in complex technological societies should be so attracted by the occasion to see themselves as naked apes, or indolent lions, or bewildered rats."[1] The Edo cartoons of small animals, like the frog, rabbit, monkey, fox, and donkey, are still used in Japanese kindergartens. Why then are these powerfully imaginative assimilations made between other species and humans to make moral conclusions about themselves? Is it not more intelligent to make comparisons among human cultures, who all have differing religions, which animals show no sign of ever having?

Expanding Horizons of Other Human Cultures

It is true that in the great period of Western discovery of other continents, in the sixteenth century, there was deep perplexity about whether their inhabitants were also human. The pious Queen Isabella sent out a Franciscan commission from Spain to find out if the Caribbean natives possessed a "soul." While the same natives were cooking their strange invaders to find out if they were edible! Seeking to know whether the natives should be emulated, or given moral sympathy, or indeed become companionable, stimulated a new form of human knowledge—ethnography, developing into anthropology, and now into cross-cultural communications. But the whole misdirection of the rise of the social sciences has been to start with the general to make generalizations about society. Instead, we should begin with the recognition that we are all unique persons, within particular cultures. Collective practices, cultural systems, and general

---

1. Rodney Needham, *Primordial Characters* (Charlottesville: University Press of Virginia, 1978), pp. 4-5.

ideologies all distort our human-ness. What is primary, are personal relationships.

I used to come to Japan with my beloved wife, but now that she has died, I have re-visited with my daughter, hoping that she, too, might be enlarged as a mother to share with other mothers. As we have recognized, being "personal" is having not a self-identity, but being "a self-for-the-other." So, this book is about "we," at many levels.

The Role of Women in Secular Cultures Today

Nothing is more socially complex today than the issue of gender equality for women. This is becoming globally so, when culturally we introduce the three broad functional categories of male/females relations as: Diomorphism, Biomorphism, and Amorphism. These incorporate all the ethnic differences of differing cultures, Western or Eastern. The traditional category of Diomorphism is when the male is occupied full-time out of the household, while the female is occupied full-time with household chores, both in the professions of cities, as well as in peasant communities with some farming activities. In Japan, the wife/mother had more dominance in the household, but the money was all in the hands of the male working outside the home.

The Biomorphic role is a newer type of equality, where the male takes more interest in child-rearing and helping around the home, as the millennial generation now does in the Westernized cultures. It reflects on urban living generally.

The Amorphic role is most recent, where the wife/mother may even be the outside worker and the male is more domesticated. Single women, as well as married ones, may decide their professional life has first priority and wait until later to have children. This would suggest greater variation of gender roles, and likewise of status roles, with more successful professional women dominating over a less intelligent/successful male spouse.

But all this social categorization does not interpret the private emotions of spouses, of their own private desires, and what their occupations force them to seek, and be. So, there is also "ambi-morphism," which reflects sharp discrepancy between what a woman privately desires and what circumstances have forced her to become. She may be more intelligent than her spouse, and finances dictate she should advance in her profession, but her traditional relatives may judge her decision critically for accepting this inverse role, or she herself would prefer, "uneconomically," to nurture her own children domestically, and forfeit her professional privileges.

Although there is much more mobility globally now for these options, some cultures still remain more traditional. Thus Japanese women probably suffer more than American women where there is still more social conservatism, especially in the rural areas. They are still haunted in their memories that "women should walk three steps behind." In conservative Kyushu, until recently, men's vests were hung *above* on the clothes line, while beneath was the clothes line for women's underwear. A revealing symbol indeed!

But all these social categories are still generalizations, which do not intimately take into account the uniquely personal suffering narrative of each woman. Certainly, the feminist movement has strengthened or weakened, according to how its protests have been vocalized politically or not. But it is Christian men who should vocalize the inequality, not lace it to a mass cultural reaction! Among Protestants there has been a weak appreciation of the adoration of the Virgin Mary, in confused reaction to her traditional idolatrous worship by many Roman Catholics, as the divine agent for the Incarnation. While the male priestly role of Roman Catholics has created great abuse in their confessional role over the intimacy of women's sexual life.

Seeking secular psycho-therapy may confuse gender equality even more, when its premise is that of Western individualism, of having "individual rights"! Again, this is not Biblical, where we are to "love one another"—the self always being for "the other." "Equality in a relationship of love" is the Christian ethic. Divorce rates dominate after child birth in the West, while it is often commoner with seniors in Japan. Both merely reflect family break-down in differing cultures. The former reflect the desire that children not being considered illegitimate. The latter express the final bitterness of Japanese older women, who were never treated with equality throughout their marriages; now they can retire with independence for the first time in their sad lives.

The Historical Heritage of *Danjyo Kankei*

Domestic language in Japan is strongly gender focused. *Danjyo* means men and women, but *Kanai,* meaning literally "inside house," refers always to women, who should be at home and obey their husbands as the superior gender.[2] But Christians, also, have long accepted male leadership, assuming "a woman's place is in the home." Only recent scholarship has shown far more evidence of gender equality in early Christianity. Likewise, in the distant past, Japan was even a matrilineal society, in which women had property rights, and there were female leaders. Emulation of the Chinese law-codes in the 6-7th centuries, and the strengthening of the rule of the Emperor by rationalizing his divine ancestry, which has only now ceased, curiously strengthened female roles. Population growth was strong because of female preference, although attacked in waves of epidemics, as in other societies. It was the opposite of China's recent disastrous demographic one-child policy, in conjunction with its social bias toward males.

Yamanoue Okura (c.660-733), an official of the court, has left us a rare poem of idyllic family life in that period; he himself is a rare example of a courtier who abandoned his official ambitions to spend more time with his family. He describes how his little son "with dawn would not leave our bed, / But standing or lying, / Played and romped with us…he would say 'Come to bed, father and mother, / Let me sleep between you.'" But alas, he was suddenly taken ill, and now the father lamented: "lacking skill and knowing no cure…lifting up my eyes to the gods in heaven, I prayed; my brow laid on the ground, I did reverence to the gods of the earth. 'Be he ill or be he well, It is in your power, O Gods.' Thus I clamored in my prayers. Yet no good came of

2. Takie Lebra, "Sex Equality for Japanese Women", in *Identity, Gender, and Status in Japan* (Folkestone, England: Global Oriental, 2007), pp. 143-152.

it, for he wasted away, each dawn he spoke less, till his life was ended...The child I held so tight has flown beyond my clasp. Is this the way of the world?"[3]

It was in the subsequent rise of the warrior states and their feudalism that the dominant role of the male took over, gradually at first, still in the regime of courtiers during the 10th-11th centuries, then violently so later, when the provincial warriors took over real governance (from the late twelfth century onwards) to create the widespread rule of the Shoguns (710-1600).[4] This led to the weakening of family bonds, for in Shogun marriages, there was no communication between husband and wife.

Commerce under the role of the emperor, who was always looking to make trade connections with the rest of the world, created a different culture. It was under this commercial prosperity that Edo, Osaka, and Kyoto all grew to have more than half a million inhabitants, even before their European counterparts. In city life, "the floating world" of cultural drama began to popularize the puppet theatre, and kabuki actresses were barely distinguishable from prostitutes. It became the "age of the geisha," first acted by males until the mid-1750s, then becoming more incorporated and widespread with women since then.[5]

A further weakening of family life has been the social and political priority given to males, in the *ie* household, that is, of extended family groupings. This tradition began

---

3. *The Japanese Mind*, ed. Roger J. Davies & Osamu Ikeno (Tokyo: Tuttle, 2002) pp. 63-4. Quoted by Kenneth Henshall, *A History of Japan* (New York: Palgrave MacMillan, 2004), pp. 20-21.

4. Ibid, pp. 23-50.

5. Ibid, p. 209, note 35.

in the "warrior" or Kamakura times (1185-1333). Much more so than in China or Korea, Japan promoted indiscriminate cultural adoption, which Japanese moralists in the nineteenth century began to deplore as cause for social chaos and lawlessness. One critic, Hozumi, believed it was derived from ancestor worship, and the stronger the belief in that practice, the more widespread it flourished.[6] The nobility practiced it more, because unlike the Emperor who had an unquestionable legacy as descended from the deity Nippon, the sun-God, the nobility rose and fell in favor at the court, according to their pedigrees. This is reminiscent of the English Tudor aristocracy of England. In Japan, it was only after World War II when universal equality and democratic principles were imposed by the Americans, that the hereditary hierarchy went out of existence.[7] Nevertheless, the basic structure of *ie* continues to persist in the urban, professionalized life today.

Family adoption, which should be motivated by human compassion, motherly instinct, the feminine desire for a child, and the well-being of other children in the family—all humane qualities—are often side-lined by the subtle, inordinate demands of social hierarchy. These weaken the ideals of a "democratic society," which cannot be imposed by such remote political organizations, such as the United Nations and its decrees, or even by local social bureaucracy

---

6. Cited by Takie Lebra, *Identity, Gender and Status in Japan* (Folkestone, Kent: Global Oriental Ltd., 2007), p. 284.
7. Ibid, p. 285.

for "family affairs." The weight of cultural heritage is still too subtle and heavy to abolish.

In more recent history, coming from a privileged status, a wife was expected to conceive sons, while daughters had to over-compensate in their careful breeding to become "proper daughters-in-a-box." They were brought up as special treasures, being praised not for their heritage but for their special grooming.[8]

"Arranged marriages," or *omiai*, as distinct from "love marriages," have long been considered as expressive of relations between one family and another, rather than just the personal choices and relations between one man and a woman. Representatives of both families controlled the couple's choices, which were highly repressed in the past. But today in the busyness of professional life, arranged marriages can become a facilitating atmosphere for couples to get to know each other, and perhaps to make wiser choices. So, according to a Ministry of Health and Welfare survey, "arranged marriages" were three times more common in 1950, but in the census of 1990 "love-marriages" had become five times more important. Ironically, the Tech Revolution in the West is now reversing trends, so that a smart phone service can organize "arranged Marriages," certainly not for "the weight" of social hierarchy, but for the opposite reason—the rise of a narcissistic culture!

At the same time, East and West, there is the other tendency to stay single, when the choice of a career and more financial freedom appear to promise a happier life. It

---

8. Roger J. Davies, *The Japanese Mind* (Hong Kong: Tuttle, 2002), p. 64-65.

may turn out to be a mirage, but then our fallen state as sinners lives on with more illusions than we ever think we have. For "open vision" requires moral freedom, especially "freedom from self," which we rarely see. Sadly, even the wives of Japanese or Western pastors quietly may complain they do not experience the same freedom to socialize as their husbands may have.

Childrearing Practices in West and Japanese *Ikuji*

The poem of the seventh-century Japanese courtier suggests there was a deeper understanding of childhood in Japanese matriarchal culture, whereas in the West, the identity of a child was distorted by the feudal aristocracy to represent the child as a miniature adult.[9] The new Romantic consciousness of Jean-Jacques Rousseau, in the eighteenth century, gave impetus to discovering the feelings of a child, in his revolutionary novel *Emile*. Pediatric education has never ceased since then. But in Japan, where more than half of communication is not verbal but imitative, child education is "seep-down parenting." By this is meant that learning is more by imitation than by explicit verbal communication, in the demonstration of the use of toys, numbers, words, and pictures. Children are rarely disciplined in punishment or other verbally authoritative ways. Instead, many strategies are used to develop inwardly a child's self-control, and

---

9. On the history of European marriage see *Histoire du Marriage,* arranged by Sabine Melchior-Bonnet and Catherine Salles (Paris: Robert Laffont, 2009).

other norms of behavior, by the social influence of classmates or siblings.

While "a good child" in America is self-assertive, having one's own opinions, and standing up for one's self, the Japanese "good child" is the opposite—non-assertive, sharing good feelings with others (*kimochi-shugi*), and being considerate of others. In a tantrum, a child kicking or slamming a door will be gently told, "the door will be crying in pain," whereas the natural reaction of a Western mother will be, "You should not do such a thing, it's naughty." School rules and parental laws operate in the West, whereas "people's feelings" dictate much more the Japanese home or school.

Social Expectations of Women in Japan (*Ryosaikenbo*)

Traditionally, the term *ryosaikenbo* meant "good wives," and "wise mothers." Introduced in the latter nineteenth century, it, too, was a period of "enlightened rule." For it had become an expectation of women to give strong and wise support to their husbands and to initiate good education of their children. Whereas in the earlier periods, wives and women generally were just to be obedient and not allowed to take initiative. Now girls were being educated as well as boys, since this progressive culture required all to contribute. In Japan's frail democracy of 1912-26, it was called the *Taisho* period, meaning "Great Righteousness." The right to vote was given to all males in 1925, while all women in America were given the vote in 1920. Yet politically this was the period of international diplomacy, when Japan had every right to complain that the West was not being consistently "righteous." There was still strong racial discrimination in the "white racial policy" of Australia, and while Japan was a founding leader in the League of Nations, the United States never formally joined. Moral inconsistencies riddle the ideals of Western democracy, in contrast to more consistency in Japanese culture.[10]

Recovering the Ethics of New Testament Family Life

As we have seen, globalization makes us all both much more cross-cultural and more seriously "historical," in the grid of both space and time. Therefore, we need also to deeply appreciate how the early Church Fathers defended the uniqueness of Christianity as their way of life, to enrich, deepen, and mature in this uniqueness. Even the ancient Greeks could distinguish between "good goddesses" such as Artemis and Athena—promoting civic culture from the erotica of Aphrodite and her nymphs. But by the early Christian era, the Caesars' wives and mistresses were involved as deeply in the politics of matricide, patricide, fratricide, and infanticide as men.[11] Paradoxically, Roman pagan "reformers" of the first century B.C. realized political sustainability depended on the family household as the central institution around which Roman civic life had to be built. Augustus focused constantly upon traditional family values, of mar-

10. Kenneth Henshall, *A History of Japan* (New York: Palgrave/Macmillan, 2004), pp. 106-110.
11. Annelise Freisenbruch, *Caesars' Wives: Sex, Power, and Politics in the Roman Empire* (New York: Free Press, 2010).

riage, child raising, and women's domestic work, in speeches and legislation. Beginning in 18 B.C.E., new laws encouraged marriage and procreation. If a freeborn woman had three children, she could be released from *tutela*, male legal guardianship, or be a freed woman for four. Undesirable sexual relationships were proscribed: freeborn men were forbidden from marrying prostitutes, adultery was proscribed, and various legal restrictions were placed on marriages between different classes.[12]

In this reformed Roman culture of the "family households," masculinity and femininity were not fixed in the way we distinguish them today as dichotomous, biological terms. But gender was seen as a model of two dynamic, interacting frameworks: a cosmic hierarchy and a regulation of desire. As Swancutt observes: "a Greek or Roman woman was by definition the penetrated, empty vessel that her husband filled, while the male citizen was legally free and expected to penetrate inferior sex partners: his wife, slaves, prostitutes, and occasionally actors or dancers."[13] Against such practices, the apostle Paul exhorted the Thessalonians: "It is God's will that you should be sanctified: that you should avoid sexual immorality; that each of you should learn to control his own body in a way that is holy and honorable, not in passionate

---

12. Carolyn Osiek and Jennifer Pouya, "Constructions of Gender in the Roman Imperial World" in *Understanding the Social World of the New Testament,* ed. Dietmar Neufeld and Richard E. DeMaris (Abingdon, Oxon, New York: Routledge, 2010), p. 44.

13. Diana Swancutt, "Sexy Stoics and the Re-reading of Romans 1:18-2:16" in Amy-Jill Levine and Marianne Blickenstaff, ed. *A Feminist Companion to Paul* (Cleveland, Oh.: Pilgrim Press, 2004, pp. 42-73).

lust like the heathen, who do not know God" (1 Thess. 4:3-5).

In the two Pauline passages of 1 Corinthians 11:2-16, about women's head-covering, and 14:34-35, about women's silence, much confusion in commentaries still exists. First, with Origen we should see the context of the apostle addressing immature Christians, dealing with problematic behavior that might scandalize the social decorum of the surrounding pagan society. He is concerned about public honor and shame in that society. There is probably a word-play with the Greek word *kephale* ("head") in verses 5 and 10, where Paul is exhorting a woman to have authority over her own head, dressing it appropriately, not disgracefully in the norms of the culture.[14] The silence demanded in 1 Corinthians 14: 34,35 is again a matter of public decorum, perhaps against ecstatic utterance, or other forms of social disturbance that will bring shame on their spouses. Again, women's proper dress and decorum are the issues of 1 Timothy 2:9-15, primarily in public but also in private settings.[15]

Similar admonitions might be made today, to overseas missionaries in Japan, not behaving wisely in adjusting to Japanese rules of etiquette, but being socially offensive to the prevailing culture.

Instead, the apostle would persuade us all to forget our cultural/historical differences, to become a "new creation" now being revealed "in Christ." Paul recites to the Galatian Christians his own past narrative and identity, demonstrat-

---

14. Carolyn Osiek and Jennifer Pouya, *Understanding the Social World of the New Testament*, op. cit., pp .48-49.

15. Ibid, pp,.50-52.

ing for the Galatians, as for himself personally, the futility of reverting to the past, or to allow it to linger on. So in Galatians 4 he explores their new freedom in Christ. It is deliverance from the past legalism of Judaism, if a Jew, or from idols, if a Gentile (vv. 1-11); it is a change that his visit with them has brought through his teaching to know and to call God, "Father" (vv. 12-20).

Southern Galatia had been "Romanised," and northern Galatia remained more anciently "native" in its ethnicity, both subsequently "Judaised," but Paul, in his two missionary journeys, speaks first against all levels of separateness when he calls upon all Christians to practice their "New Humanity." He writes:

> You are all sons of God through faith in Christ Jesus, for all of you who were baptized into Christ have clothed yourselves with Christ. There is neither Jew nor Greek, slave nor free, male or female, for you are all one in Christ Jesus. If you belong to Christ, then you are Abraham's seed, and heirs according to the promise (Galatians 3:26-29).

It remains for all of us an inconceivable freedom, an echo of what Jesus promised "to those who believed in him":

> If you hold to my teaching, you are really my disciples. Then you will know the truth and the truth will set you free.... I tell you the truth, everyone who sins is a slave to sin. Now a slave has no permanent place in the fam-

ily, but a son belongs to it forever. So if the Son makes you free, you will be free indeed (Jn. 8:31-32, 34-36).

This meant that in the rise of Christianity there was a profound transformation of humanity, dissolving all traditional systems, whether Jewish or pagan, dissolute or moral, within the freedom of divine "sonship" that is neither male or female, since gender and sex are but creaturely things. The letter to the Galatians likewise is the voice for freedom—freedom from the worship of "nature," as forms of idolatry; freedom from the law, as forms of religious immaturity; freedom from self, which is "slavery to the flesh," in whatever form "selfism" may take.

4

Personal Emotions—Classical, Japanese, Western, and Christian

Far more profoundly than we may realize, human emotions shape our world. With Climate Change we already fear the human impact on our planet earth. With the substitution of artificial intelligence for our human intelligence, great new forces of fear will be shortly released. Among these is the fear of the loss of jobs, or of the loss of privacy, as no systems of email security can guarantee to guard our intimate communications. Geo-politics today between nations are all grounded upon fear, so that the more political dictators seek control—to have unsurpassed power, to become gods of power—the more they are themselves filled with fear.[1]

---

1. Dominique Moisi, *Geopolitics of Emotion, How Cultures of Fear, Humiliation, and Hope are Re-Shaping the World* (New York: Anchor Books, Random Press, 2009).

Neuroscientists now inform us that fear is our basic human emotion, located in the lower thalamus of the brain.[2]

Fear, the Basic Human Emotion

"What is emotion?" To answer this is like the proverbial five blind men describing an elephant. Neuroscientists will describe how the human brain is wired to communicate emotions, primarily of fear. The pediatrician will begin with the bonding of an infant to its mother, which then causes early fears in the child. The geriatric psychiatrist will focus on the emotions of the ending of human life. It is not surprising, then, that when we study and compare human cultures we find the same elemental characteristic of fear in every human culture, re-shaped, re-defined, re-expressed in diverse ways, dependent upon its history, geography, and human adaptations.

Considering eastern Asia alone, fear is intense in Korea, with strong fears against all kinds of evil spirits, because it is a small state(s) between the much stronger nations of China and Japan. As a sub-continental civilization, China's basic fears are internalized and hierarchical, directed upwards towards the Emperor and "Heaven." With insularity, Japan's fears are internalized downwards, with deep social fears of not being excluded within a strongly-knit culture.

Biblically however, "God is love" and "love is of God" (1 Jn. 4:7). "There is no fear in love, but perfect love casts out all fear" (1 Jn. 4:18). "Sin" is the Biblical cause of "fear," as when Adam and Eve hid themselves in the garden of

---

2. D. Theodore George, *Untangling the Mind: Why We Behave the Way We Do* (New York: Harper Collins, 2013).

temptation. This is the fear of being alienated from God and his love; we are all sinners, thus always motivated by fear in multiple ways. This explains the most intimate personal behavior, and yet also the motives of fear behind the new "cold war" that chillingly threatens the future of the human race on planet earth. Ironically, man can more easily explore the solar system and even plan human colonies on distant planets than resolve peace in the Middle East among hostile ethnic groups. Haunted by fear, the human race has no future without God. But by beginning to re-frame it all as the behavior of sinners, we take the first step towards God's redemptive future.

Again, without God our experience of "love" can be profoundly deceitful. I have met some people who have had horrendous childhoods of parental neglect and abuse, totally deprived of love. Yet they have reacted so strongly that they attempt to create love all around them. Literally, they create themselves as their own "savior," by radiating kindness around themselves. Socially they are most endearing, as "angels of light," yet they are so profoundly deceitful. For "God" and "sin" are not in their understanding of the human condition.

Rather we are arguing that our human condition, as emotional beings, can only be understood and redeemed by relating all our emotions before God and his multiple emotions towards us.

Who Is God among the "Gods"?

Japanese society is still deeply idolatrous, in spite of its Western secularism. Yet all human beings are worshippers of some "thing," or some "god." Who then is God among "the gods"? God is the primordial reality who created the cosmos "ex nihilo," out of nothing before "nature" ever existed, whereas Buddhism and Platonism have both started with "nature" as their primordial reality. As we noted, the great physicist Einstein marveled that the greatest mystery of the universe is its comprehensibility by the human mind, whom God created. So, our minds and wills reach out to his incomprehensibility.

Yet God is also more inward to me than any self-knowledge, as Psalm 139 so profoundly explores God's intimate knowledge of who I am, where I came from, where I am going. "Such knowledge is too wonderful for me," the psalmist can only respond. So, he concludes, "Search me, O God, and know my heart! Try me and know my thoughts! And see if there be any grievous way in me, and lead me in the way everlasting" (Psalm 139:6, 24). The Biblical prophets expose, then, the folly of idolatry that it is all man-made, whose worship is really only self-worship, since humans have created their own gods, whom they now fear (Isaiah 44:9-20).

In his own long search for God, Augustine, with all his brilliance of mind, recognized God is not only *superior summo meo*—beyond my utmost heights of intellect and will—but also *interior intimo meo,* that is, more inward to me than my inmost depths of emotions and feelings. No idolatrous religion can ever make such claims.

Likewise, no absolutely convinced atheist can fail to recognize that he/she has set a boundary to what a human being can know. But God is not limited like human beings, so the adopted ignorance of atheism is no different from savages on an isolated island having no awareness nor interest in another continent. Even a brilliant scientist can take this posture, that beyond my thinking there is nothing else that is thinkable, even if the power of the scientific mind lies in always asking more questions![3] We then associate or even create a community to think like us, even a brilliant scientific community. Always we need the reminder that our ways of seeing the world and of seeing other people may not be as the world and other people truly are!

Biblical Foundations of the Human Emotions

The first great Biblical scholar, Origen, as he prepared to write his commentary on Genesis, begins with great humility: "Like the one who has set out on a sea in a small boat is filled with immense anxiety, as he is entrusting a small piece of wood to the immensity of the waves, so also we are apprehensive as we venture into such a vast ocean of mysteries."[4] But the Buddhist mythology of penetrating into "Nature" is for the human to become deified as gods, no longer human and therefore no longer with human emotions, for "gods" as idols have no emotions.

In contrast, the Biblical Creator, in contemplating his work of creation, first expresses aesthetic delight with his creation as being "good," or beautiful (*tob*). In each act of creating order in the midst of chaos, the divine pronouncement is made six times: "God saw it was good." Then, after creating man in his image and likeness, he saw it was very

---

3. See David Bentley Hart, *The Experience of God: Being, Consciousness, Bliss* (New Haven/London: Yale University Press, 2013), pp. 13-45.
4. Origen, pp. 12, 210.

good (Gen. 1). There is no other literature so ancient and so rich in expressing all the emotions than the Bible—so immensely rich about God, and also about human emotions.

"Emotions" are what move us (Latin *movere*)—profoundly moving our inner being. Uniquely the Biblical God is "personal," so a vast range of metaphorical emotions "move" God: anger, hatred, jealousy, repugnance, and indifference, on the dark and chaotic side of life, and love, kindness, compassion, tenderness, forgiveness, and intimacy, on the light side. Likewise, the Biblical prophets express the same depths of emotions, of darkness and light, judgments and blessings. Meeting with God, listening to his word, obeying his will, is all about transformed emotions, changing the whole life and destiny of individuals and of nations.

"Desires" are other motions of our inner being. This can be a radical power for human knowing and human relating, at all levels of our existence. It was desire that tempted the woman Eve to be as a god in tasting of the tree of good and evil, seeing it to be "good for food, a delight to the eyes, and that the tree was to be desired to make one wise" (Gen. 3:6). The Hebrew word, *hmd*, is expressive of a fundamental human condition, revealing two faces: it can be for light and life, or for death and darkness. It is therefore not just a vague feeling but the choice of life or death. Therefore the ninth and tenth commandments of the Biblical law decree: "you shall not covet/desire your neighbor's house…nor your neighbor's wife" (Exod. 20:17; Deut. 5:21). Later in the New Testament, James expands on the role played by desire (*epithymia*): "one is tempted by one's own desire, being lured and enticed by it; then, when that desire is conceived, it gives birth to sin, and that sin, when it is fully grown, gives birth to death" (James 1:14-15).

But when desire is infinite, desiring God alone, then we pray as in the Lord's prayer, "Thy Kingdom come, thy will be done on earth as it is in heaven!" (Matt. 6:33). Our Lord is repeating what the Old Testament prophets had already commanded: "Seek/desire the Lord, while He may be found!... When you search/desire the Lord He will be found! ...When you search for Me you will find me; if you seek me with all your heart, I will let you find Me, you will find Me" (Isa. 55:6; Jer. 29:13-14). So the faithful are described by Isaiah as "those who seek the Lord" (Isa. 51:1).

The main organ for Biblical emotions is the heart (*leb/lebab*), although the ear, too, has a strong relationship with God who speaks his *torah* (word). Since out of the heart are the issues of life, we are enjoined "to love the Lord our God with all our heart" (Deut. 6:5).

Numerically, then, the heart as *leb/lebab* occurs 860 times in the Old Testament and the Greek *kardia*, 156 times in the New Testament. These emotions are fully expressive, whereas in Buddhism the inexpressible emotions lie locked in the stomach, as Buddha himself with his over-sized stomach exhibits passively. The biblical "I" is correlative with the "heart," in self-communication and self-disclosure.

The revelation of divine emotions in the Old Testament appears so shocking in their fullness and range that would-be Roman reformers in early Christianity, such as Marcion, wanted to judge the Old Testament as expressive of a wicked god, while only the New Testament could be expressive of a "good God." Christians have often been caused to stumble ever since by this Marcionite contrast in morality. Marcion, as a Roman wealthy entrepreneur, was unaware he was much more a Roman Stoic than a Biblical Christian. He only allowed a limited exercise of his emotional potential. We shall explore this later.

Marcion completely overlooked the riches of emotions expressed in the oldest literary document, the Psalms, traceable back three millennia or more, that is to the Iron Age. Later Athanasius was to describe the Psalms as the Bible in miniature, while many Fathers of the Church have seen the *torah*, or Biblical scriptures, as "enfleshed," because of the whole range of emotions they encompass. Buddhist scriptures are wholly lacking in any human emotions. Set to music, expressed in poetry, memorized in thought, containing clarification of vices and virtues, the Psalms conclude "let everything that has breath praise the Lord!" (Psalm 150:6). The Psalms are fully, ethically transformative, out of God's intent to make us genuinely human beings.[5] Later, John Calvin, like many before him, was to experience the Psalms "to be an anatomy of all parts of the soul," adding "for there is not an emotion of which any can be conscious that is not here represented as in a mirror. Or rather, the Holy Spirit has here drawn to the life all the griefs, sorrows, fears, doubts, hopes, cares, and perplexities with which the minds of men are wont to be agitated."[6] Thus do the Psalms set our

---

5. See Gordon J. Wenham, *Psalms as Torah: Reading Biblical Songs Ethically* (Grand Rapids, Michigan: Baker Academic, 2012).

6. John Calvin, Commentary on the Psalms, preface.

hearts—with all their desires and emotions— aflame in the love of God, free indeed from fear.

Christian Versus Buddhist Emotions

Buddha was a very different prophet, and was no psalmist whatsoever, compared to the Biblical writers. Japanese culture is still strongly "religious," in spite of a veneer of contemporary secularism, in its Buddhist and later Shinto expressions. While these dominate over more primitive animism, the latter, too, is not eliminated. If the engagement is New Testament Christianity versus Buddhism, then Buddha precedes Christ by several hundred years.[7] But the Biblical claim is that Christianity is rooted in the whole span of Judaism, when Israel was called to be the covenant people of God. Thus we contrast the whole of the Biblical Scriptures of the Old and the New Testament with the Buddhist texts. Particularly we may contrast them with the later Old Testament prophets, as the contemporaries of Buddha.

From this Buddhist source, personal emotions in Japan still show strong restraint because of the pessimistic worldview of Buddhism, and the aristocratic, military Shinto culture promoted in the Edo period of 1600 to 1867, and again during the military campaigns in the 1930s to 1945. Whereas, as we have seen, Biblical emotions are extraordi-

---

7. Most scholars would date the birth of Buddha about 566 B.C.E. and his death c.486 B.C.E. South East Asian scholars push it further back to 624-544 B.C.E., while many Japanese scholars put it forward to 448-368 B.C.E. See Leo D. Lefebure, *The Buddha and Christ* (Maryknoll, New York, 1993), p. 5.

narily rich, based upon the God of the cosmos, who is the source of love—indeed, he *is* love.

Stoicism, East and West

True, Stoicism has often intermingled with Biblical emotions, as Christianity encountered and challenged the Roman civilization, which became increasingly "Stoical" towards its final collapse. Stoicism has been a haunting recurrence at various periods of Western history. Hence it cannot be overlooked within our Christian "history." As the poet T. S. Eliot has noted: "Stoicism is the refuge for the individual in an indifferent or hostile world too big for him; it is the permanent substratum of a number of versions of cheering oneself up; it is the reverse of humility."[8] Essentially, Stoicism, East or West, is expressive of cultures of "fear," and of their human responses.

There are many expressions of Buddhist stoicism, but the primary source in Japan is Zen-Buddhism. Its wisdom

---

8. T.S. Eliot, "Shakespeare and the Stoicism of Seneca," in *Selected Essays* (London: Faber & Faber, 1949), pp. 131-32.

is expressed in a four-line stanza transmitted first from India into China, and then later into Japan. It is:

> "A special transmission outside the scriptures,
> Not founded upon words and letters;
> By pointing directly to [one's] mind
> It lets one see into [one's own true] nature and [thus] Attain Buddhahood."

The deepest expressions of Buddhist wisdom are silence, the antithesis of Biblical prophecy. Buddhists tell us the Buddha taught 80,000 doctrines but never said a word, yet the Buddha spent about 45 years preaching out of compassion for all living things. Buddhism is little practiced in India, its birthplace, but as a missionary movement it is widely spread through eastern Asia, with considerably differing regional diversities. Extending now into the Western world, it does call for dialogue, concerning its claims of transformation of the human believer, and the efficacy of human emotions. Yet it denies the existence of an independent, permanent self, as a radical counterpoint and challenge to Christian identity as being personal in a personal God.

Contrastively, Buddhist silence extends to the existence of God, which Westerns can only interpret as expressing a form of atheism. Buddhism also denies creation, speaking instead of dependent co-existing, as having no cosmological explanation about the universe.[9] Modern science could never have arisen from this Buddhist heritage, so why continue

---

9. Ibid, p. xx.

being a Buddhist in modern Japanese society, when the society is now so dependent on modern science for its survival?

Such, then, is the impasse between Buddhism and Christianity, that there can only be two approaches. As a scholar studying comparative religion, one can detach one's self as a secularist, being neither Buddhist nor Christian, remaining as a critical outsider, as an atheist might be. Or else, as a simple Japanese Christian sharing the same paddy fields as one's Buddhist neighbors, one simply expresses one's faith in "being a Christian," with loving emotions. What kind of "silence" is then being exchanged? Is it alienating or is it loving? Is the common suffering of being human somehow being expressed differently?

This profound religious encounter actually promotes "bedrock" convictions of faith, faith for which one is prepared passionately to die for. Then a hymn such as we may sing familiarly in church worship becomes a daily, domestic reality:

> "On Christ the solid Rock I stand,
> All other ground is sinking sand."

Yet such a profound challenge requires Christians to become ever deeper in their intelligence, as in their emotions, so that the reformed command to the Israelites is obeyed by us also:

> Hear O Israel: the Lord is One. Love the Lord your God with all your heart and with all your soul, and with all your strength… impress them on your children. Talk about them when you sit at home and when you walk along the road, when you lie down and when you get up. Tie them as symbols on your hands and

bind them on your foreheads. Write them on the doorframes of your houses and on your gates (Deut. 6:4-9).

For like no other religion, Biblical faith is domesticated, with worship being centered in the home, not in a temple for idol worship. All other religions are in temples made with hands, with idols made of stone, with religious rites carried out by priests.

Stoicism, East or West, Is Self-Containment

It may appear paradoxical that in the midst of an idolatrous culture, one can also be inwardly self-contained. Yet the Greeks, surrounded by their gods, explored Stoicism deeply. Like the Buddhist teaching, Greek Stoicism saw the whole cosmos as a simple unity, material in nature, yet also deified as "Nature." But Man as above the animals has more than an instinctual life for self preservation; he has the moral impulse to be oneself, or *oikeiosis*. This has three stages: (1) being self-conscious; (2) having a natural love of self; and (3) being attached to oneself.[10] The Greek Stoics were thus more individuated than Buddhist stoicism. They were also more rational, and as the apostle Paul debates with both Stoics and Epicureans on Mars Hill, the Stoics were more "reasonably open" to hear what the apostle had to communicate (Acts 17:18). But the apostle was profoundly anti-Stoic in his Christian message that all humanity are called to be "in Christ" and not in themselves. This is the heart of all his epistles, that "to be in Christ is a new creation." Some

10. Troels Engberg-Pedersen, *The Stoic Theory of Oikeiosis* (Aarhus, Denmark: Aarhus University Press, 1990), pp. 64-71.

166 times, this identity of the Christian is used by the great Christian missionary.

Contemporary with the apostle Paul was the great Roman statesman Seneca, whose cultivation of a harmonious personality is also seen in the contemporary practice of much psychotherapy. He taught:

> I shall tell you what I mean by health: if the mind is content with its own self; if it has confidence in itself; if it understands that all those things for which men pray, all the benefits which are bestowed and sought for, are of no importance in relation to a life of happiness; under such conditions it is sound. The effect of wisdom is a joy that is unbroken and continuous. The mind of the wise is like the ultra-lunar firmament; eternal calm pervades that region, it is consistent with itself throughout.[11]

Writing to his young friend Lucilius, Seneca further defines Stoic joy: "Take joy only in that which comes from your own. What do I mean by *what is your own*? I mean you yourself and your own best part."[12] Again the apostle Paul is so contrastive, experiencing joy as always relational, as always being in the presence of Christ, as always shared with others, never a solitary joy, but always a social joy.[13] This is where

---

11. Jan N. Sevenster, *Paul and Seneca* (Leiden: E.J.Brill, 1961), p. 107.

12. Cited by Martha C. Nussbaum, *The Therapy of Desire* (Princeton: Princeton University Press, 1994), p. 400.

13. See my summary of Stoicism versus Christian faith, James M. Houston, *The Mentored Life: from Individualism to Personhood* (Vancouver: Regent College Publishing, 2012), pp. 57-79.

Japanese Christians can exercise their cultural heritage of "belonging,"[14] now not to themselves, but as being "found of Christ," "called by Christ," "following Christ." Psalm 1 describes stoicism—without using the name—as "the way of the wicked," and it is what the Bible means by "sin."

Contemporary psycho-therapy is all about Stoicism. For it is what sustains Secularism, East and West. It is all about being one's own god, one's own redeemer, one's own emotional resource. The consequence emotionally is that there is no future, only the present moment which I can grasp as my momentary happiness, as is so visually apparent in the Japanese mountains, where the temples are built as the realm of the gods. One lives below that realm, much more so in the forests, with their very limited horizons, or work in the paddy fields as small clearances among the trees.[15] For the Greeks and Romans, as for the Japanese culture, "the present alone is our happiness."[16] For the future is not ours to control. Only "in Christ" is there a future—a glorious future!

---

14. A contemporary handbook on such psycho-therapy is Donald Robertson, *Stoicism and the Art of Happiness* (London: Hodder & Stoughton, 2013).

15. See Robert Pogue Harrison, *Forests: the Shadow of Civilization* (Chicago & London: The Chicago University Press, 1992).

16. Pierre Hadot, *The Present Alone is our Happiness*, trans. Marc Djaballah & Michael Chase (Stanford: Stanford University Press, 2011), pp. 162-74.

5

Core Cultural Values of Relationship—Contexts of Friendship and Community, Japanese and Western

A test of the uniqueness of a culture is evidenced by the distinctive words that are most commonly used. Japan is no exception. Such words carry far more meaning than other words translated into other languages. For example, *Giri* is the whole world of Japanese social obligations, while *Amae* is the realm of Japanese social dependence. Western languages also carry their own history, but not with such depths and range of human emotions, as just these two Japanese words. This seems paradoxical, when we have noted how Japanese appear publicly to be so emotionally stoic. Yet all words, Japanese or English, are culture-laden, making translation always a challenge.

    Automatic technology that translates electronically can efficiently communicate news or business affairs from another language, but no effort is made to enter the depth of a culture, its history and religious traditions. It is merely encoding information, promoting data processing with a talking machine. It is designative, not constitutive language, as Charles Taylor has recently explored.[1] But when language is shared cross-culturally, we find that cross-cultural linguistics is rich in exchanging cultural differences, to enhance our humanity. Secularism ignores cultures, in denying their religious origins, so it can never be human enough; it cannot defend us from becoming hominids, as we concluded in our second essay. Instead, we shall now see how rich Japanese culture is in being relational and how it can significantly enrich Western culture, which is now becoming so much more secularized.

The Basis of Japanese Relational Life

The Japanese psychiatrist Takeo Doi has pioneered the theme that *amae* is "a peculiarly Japanese emotion," and is "a thread that runs through all the various activities of Japanese society."[2] In his voluminous writings, he has shown that no comparable single English word exists, with so many explications. Even the Japanese dictionary has several definitions, such as, "to lean on a person's good will," or "to depend on another's affection."[3] *Amaeru*, the intransitive verb form of *amae*, means "to depend and to presume upon another's benevolence," and is expanded to denote helplessness as a

---

1. Charles Taylor, *The Language Animal* (Boston: Harvard University Press, the Belknap Press, 2016), pp. 1-50.
2. Takeo Doi, *The Anatomy of Dependence* (Tokyo: Kodansha, 1981), pp. 169, 26.
3. Ibid, pp. 72, 167.

baby, yet also a child spoilt indulgently.[4] In his foreword to this classic study, John Bester argues that *amae* is thus the prototype of what every normal baby feels at the breast of its mother—dependence, the desire to be passively loved, the unwillingness to be separated from the warmth and nurture of the mother and be brought into the harsh reality of the objective world that entails separation.[5]

No other Japanese word, concept, or attitude can more powerfully challenge Western cultures than *amae*. In contrast, to our "ego-culture," perhaps most exaggerated in the United States, a good dose of *amae* would be culturally beneficial. For American culture promotes the autonomous self, the self-expanding self, the assertive and competitive self, the contractual and leadership self, and even the empty-self, as its consumers flock to the shopping malls with credit cards, eager to participate in the cult of self-fulfillment. Japanese psychotherapist Takao Murase, in advocating more of the spirit of *Sunao*, that is, of being gentle and obedient, does not go nearly far enough in his application of *amae*.[6] Not surprisingly, Japanese often find Westerns emotionally immature and rude. Western Christians should also seriously explore *amae* for Christian relationships, at all lev-

---

4. Anna Wierzbicka, *Understanding Cultures Through Their Key Words* (Oxford/ New York: Oxford University Press, 1997, University Press), p. 237.

5. John Bester, *Foreword,* Ibid, p. 8.

6. Takao Murase, *"Sunao:* a Central Concept in Japanese Psycho-Therapy" in Marsella, Anthony and White, Geoffrey, eds., *Cultural Conceptions of Mental Health and Therapy* (Dordrecht: Reidel, 1984, (pp. 317-329).

els. For it is the infant loss of basic trust that keeps so many multitudes skeptical of God's existence and of his love.

In converse, it is the absence/disbelief of the biblical application of *amae* that needs to be vocalized and witnessed: "Can a mother forget the baby at her breast and have no compassion on the child she has borne? Though she may forget, I will not forget you! You, I have engraved you on the palms of my hands" (Isa. 49: 15-16). "But I have stilled and quieted my soul; like a weaned child with its mother, like a weaned child is my soul within me" (Ps. 131:2). Again, "Though my father and mother forsake me, the Lord will receive me" (Ps. 27:10). Such basic trust is foundational to all subsequent human behavior and for all human relations.

Other Japanese Premises for Human Relationships

The Japanese term *Wa*, usually translated as "harmony," is as basic, humanly, in Japanese culture as Biblically we may use the word "righteousness." Anna Wierzbicka cites Kokutai no Hongi, in this regard:

> When we trace …the progress of our history, what we always find there is the spirit of harmony. Harmony is a product of the great achievements of the founding of the nation, and is the power behind our historical growth; while it is also a humanitarian Way inseparable from our daily lives…our country makes harmony its fundamental Way. Herein lies the reason why the

ideologies of our nation are different from those of the nations of the West.[7]

Wa used in the secular meaning of "integrity" has also been admired by Western business leaders. A pre-war nationalist pamphlet, *Principles of the National Polity*, contrasts Western individualism with the central value of *wa*: "In individualism there can exist co-operation, compromise, self-sacrifice, and so on… but in the final analysis there is no real harmony (*wa*)… Not conflicts, but harmony is final."[8] *Wa* then, as harmony within a group, as in the nation, is a key value. Yet, like all human societies, it is not actualized, but desired and aimed for. Like our universal desire for peace, it is a dream more than a reality. What *wa* does maintain is the existential distinction between I and Thou, which is so much blurred in Western individualism.

How deep then is the need of "harmony" in the human being. The neuro-scientist Iain McGilchrist, has noted that while it is conventional wisdom to locate linguistic capacity in the left hemisphere of the brain—in the parietal region—it is within the right hemisphere that the grasping of meanings in sentences takes place, within a realm he concludes is for music, harmony, and synthesis.[9] For language

---

7. Anna Wierzbicka, *Understanding Cultures, op. cit.*, p. 248.

8. Ibid, p. 249

9. Iain McGilchrist, *The Master and his Emissary: the Divided Brain and the Making of the Western World* (New Haven, Connect.: Yale University Press, 2009), pp. 99ff.

then to evolve from music suggests the role of *wa* in Japanese culture is ancient indeed!

On is another primary term, referring to the response in being granted a favor. Like medieval society in the West, it was repaying a fief by military service, or more generally today being grateful for a gift being given. "Gratitude," however, is too inactive, requiring something more tangible. To respond to it as receiving God's blessing is therefore too foreign culturally to be conceived as such a divine bestowal. Rather, Japanese grounds "gratitude" as only humanly responsive in loyalty, devotion, having good feelings, and yet humanly burdened by a sense of obligation, in "debts" small and large. Deeply this humanistic psyche inhibits the acceptance of "the gift of the Holy Spirit" (Acts 2:38), or of thanking God "for his unspeakable gift" (2 Cor. 9.15). The numerous times the apostle expresses gratitude for "the gift of righteousness," and "the gift of life" is distinctive to Eastern religions. Contrastively, in Buddhism, as in other Asian religions, gifts from the gods always require religious actions, rites, obligations for these blessings, or *Hoon*. This too, is the origin of the culture of filial piety, as the early Buddhist work *Anguttara Nikaya* expresses:

> We may carry our mothers on one shoulder, and our fathers on the other, and attend on them even for a hundred years, doing them bodily service in every possible way, and establishing them in the position of uni-

versal sovereignty: still the favor we have received from our parents will be far from requited.[10]

It is essentially contractual, never the reception of unconditional love.

As any international business leader knows, the whole world of Japanese trade revolves around another key term, *Giri*. It is not Western integrity that provides sustainability of commerce, but Japanese *giri*, which encompasses justice, honor, propriety, rectitude, courtesy, decency, and moral cause. It is more like Kant's abstract moral imperative. *Giri* is then the linchpin of human relations among Japanese. It is the closest relationship one can have with another individual, interacting face to face.

An early source of *giri* was the ancient custom of the peasant rice cultivators needing at certain times of the growing season to have the close co-operation of neighbors mutually helping each other. Living together in small hamlets, helping mutually in the planting and harvesting seasons, reciprocal goodwill was easily checked, expected, and rewarded. It was a utilitarian exchange of "loving your neighbor," each mutually helping the other. Significantly, on mounds above the rice fields even today are the burial plots of ancestors with shrines for ancestor worship and the ongoing culture of filial piety. All the landscape communicates *giri*!

Clearly, there have been many more changes in the social expectations of *giri*, which require reciprocity, which strangers or those caught up in changing culture are not aware of. This puts strains on incipient friendships. Likewise,

---

10. Robert Bellah, *Tokugawa Religion: The Cultural Roots of Modern Japan* (New York: Free Press, 1985).

more primitive societies in rural Japan still practice compulsory gifts, while those in the cities are modified by the levels of cross-cultural interactions.

The more self-conscious one may be about *giri*, the more burdensome it is to carry out. Thus relations with in-laws are often strained, because they are called "relatives-in-*giri*"; at all costs, one must avoid the dreaded condemnation: "he does not know *giri*."[11] In her classic *The Chrysanthemum and the Sword*, Ruth Benedict reviews deeply the whole culture of *giri*, as the core of the Japanese culture, and as a major source of its profound social fear; the loss of *amae* being the other. Clearly, there are many other distinctive Japanese social terms, but these described are the pivotal ones.

Cross-Cultural Friendships

Multiple factors distinguish such variants of "friendship." From what we have described of Japanese relationships, friendship appears in low key because of inadequate social reciprocity. Intimacy of friendship *(shinyu)* is gender divided, male with male, female with female. Small children are not expected to have such intimacy, so the loose word *tomodachi* is used. In work, friendly relations are called *doryo*, but only those of the same rank in the business. A group of friends, with whom one is simply "friendly," is called *nakama*, while *nominakama* refers to the drinking friends of city commuters, delaying the return home after work-hours.

---

11. Ruth Benedict, *The Chrysanthemum and the Sword* (London: Secker & Warburg, 1953), p. 133.

Ironically a man may often share more intimacy with his drinking friends than with his own wife and family.

In China, the density of its long history and vast extent have generated a sequence of new acquaintances being passed down in a series of recommendations, so that newcomers are processed from one level of social acceptance to another. Only then may the outsider eventually become favorably acceptable into increasingly more intimate relationships. But a long duration of family connections is required to achieve such intimacy.

The term "friend" is much more generally used in the West, without such subtle undertones as in Eastern Asia. Some cultures are more "needy" of friendship, especially those more dominated by external fears, such as Russian friendship, under the oppression of the Czars and contemporary dictatorship. Hedrick Smith, in his study *The Russians,* has noted that close friendships, i.e., *drug*, are made for self-preservation, for it is in the threat of the betrayal of confidences that they are highly selective.[12] These require total commitment, which appear almost exhaustive to those coming from an open democracy. But the need to release pent-up feelings becomes very real indeed. For such friendship, the word *drug* has very high frequency of expression, such as we have seen with the Japanese term *amae*.

Greatly contrastive is the use of the Australian term "mate," which so loosely refers to a friend. But then Australia is a vast semi-desert continent, with no fear of the Aborigines as the original inhabitants. Favored, too, by convict settlers from England, the social dregs of its society, social horizon-

---

12. Hedrick Smith, *The Russians* (London: Sphere Books, *1976).*

tality was early assumed and accepted. Spending a lot of time together, getting things done together, and drinking together have become a cultural norm. Strongly chauvinistic, "clever Sheila" has had to be tough, with little feminine gentleness, the antithesis of her Japanese female. Mates are like each other, level with each, working with each other, as non-intimate "friends."[13]

Western Sources for Friendship

But these cultural differences of friendship today are philosophically shallow compared to the deep sources of Western culture. In the Homeric epic poems, the *Iliad* and *Odyssey*, at the dawn of Western culture, Odysseus was an exemplar, expected to love (*philein*) all within his extended household, and any admitted guests. "As always, god brings like and like together," was a premise for such mutuality of relationship. Then dating from the 6th to 5th century B.C., the *Theognis* suggests that there is no greater human quality than trustworthiness, exercising wisdom in choosing good and not bad friendships, doing so not for erotic passion (*eros*) but for good reason (*philia*).[14] Unpossessive love in friendship is then discussed by Socrates (c.469-399 B.C.) as desiring to give happiness to the beloved. This theme is expanded by his disciple Plato (427-327 B.C.) into giving ascent in friendship towards beauty and goodness also.[15] But here *philia* is

---

13. Ponch Hawkes, *Best Mates* (Melbourne: McPhee Gribble, 1990).
14. Liz Carmichael, *Friendship: Interpreting Christian Love* (London: T.& T. Clark, 2007), pp. 8-9.
15. Plato, *Phaedrus*, trans. Robin Waterfield (Oxford: Oxford University Press, 2009).

becoming more restrictive as male to male, rather than both sexes. Independent in thought, his pupil Aristotle (384-322 B.C.) links friendship as both for the lives of individuals and for the political community of the city-state as well. In the *Nichomachaen Ethics,* he distinguishes three categories of friendship for three separate goals: the good, the pleasant, and the useful, which are complete or perfect, or are partners for advantage/ pleasure, or are utilitarian, such as are business partners.[16]

In Hellenistic or Roman thought, excellence was recognized in wisdom, in being wholly self-sufficient, while friendships could now be between powerful patrons and inadequate partners. Withdrawn from political life, the Epicureans sought friendships more for community and mindful quests. But Cicero (106-43 B.C.), as a Stoic, wrote a classic on friendship, entitled "De Amicitia," that has remained profoundly influential on Western cultures ever since. He argued that friendship fits perfectly with our human nature, having a noble origin of love for love's sake. Such friends will grow in goodness and yet will be challenged by ethical difficulties, over choosing and losing friends, having the right kind of self-love, and serving both the interests of the community and of the individual. Seneca (4 B.C.-65 A.D.), another Stoic, as a philosophical evangelist of friendship, states men are the children of god, who should actively choose friends.[17] Epictetus (c.50-130 A.D.), a freed slave understood god as being "personal," stating boldly: "I am a free man and a friend of god, so as to obey him of my

16. Aristotle, *Nichomachean Ethics.*
17. Seneca, *Dialogues and Letters,* ed. & trans. C.D.N. Costa (London/ New York: , Penguin Books, 1997).

own free will."[18] Plutarch (c.50-120, A.D.) concludes that friendship should also be with one's wife, provided she is as educated as her spouse! For he saw that "frank speech" was also the exercise of friendship.[19]

Christian Love Is Not Classical Friendship

Just as constitutive language can describe Japanese terms such as *giri* and *amae,* so Greek terms *eros* and *philia* are the same. The use of the mind is universal in permitting us to use constitutive language as translatable factually, but it cannot convey the appropriate emotions used within a culture. Christian thought, like Greek thought, or Japanese thought, can share concepts and their differences, but these do not universally convey the emotions and desires a culture is nurtured to promote. So with regard to classical friendship, A. Nygren was right to protest that the New Testament Greek word *agape* means infinitely more than neighborly charity when it is used of God's love for humanity in the gift of his Son... "God so loved the world that He gave his own Son"(Jn. 3:16).[20] Biblical love is God's love for humanity, rather than all human efforts to generate and exercise love. Our love for God is essentially accepting the gift of his love, whereby to love him, as well as our neighbor. Its source is "in God the Father," always "from God the Son," and "by God the Holy Spirit" (2 Corinthians, 13,14). *Agape* is then almost entirely absent from all Greek philosophy and infre-

18. Epictetus, *Discourses V, iii,* 9.
19. E.N. O'Neill, "Plutarch on Friendship," in J.T. Fitzgerald (ed.) *Graeco-Roman Perspectives,* pp. 105-22.
20. A. Nygren, *Agape and Eros* (London: Faber & Faber, 1953).

quent in classical literature.[21] Whereas the New Testament literature is motivated and fully expressive of *philia* and *agape*. Addressing a Greek audience, Luke begins his Gospel and Acts to *Theophilos*, perhaps a personal friend, but generically also used as the title of all Christians: "a beloved," "lover," "friend of God."

Throughout the centuries, great Christians have radiated their experiences as "the friends of God," which one group in the late-thirteenth century called themselves, as they traded in the Rhineland valley. The lives of such Christians were shaped by having stimulating friends, in commerce, in the court, in village communities, and in all environmental and social conditions. Literature about them all is inexhaustible, but my own friend Liz Carmichael has given a wonderful historical synopsis of interpreting Christian love through history.[22] My own summary of the Christian's exercise of prayer is as a "transforming friendship."[23]

In contrast to the Biblical source of Christ's commandment to "love one another as I have loved you," which is sourced in God's gift of love to us, Japanese *giri* is sourced in social law, as the Tokugawa rule of the Edo Period (1603-1868), *shusigaku giri* came to mean a rule one has to obey in human relations.[24]

Again the Japanese culture of giving as *giri* is now interpreted by neuro-scientists as a basic feature of the human

---

21. A.H. Armstrong & R.A. Markus, *Christian Faith and Greek Literature* (London: Darton Longman & Todd, Ltd.), p. 80.

22. Liz Carmichael, *Friendship, op. cit.*

23. James M. Houston, *The Transforming Friendship* (Vancouver, Canada: Regent College Publishing, 1996, 2007).

24. *Japanese History* (Tokyo: Bilingual Books, 1996), p. 97.

brain, functioning for our well-being as a source of happiness. Anthropologists have long been aware of how the diverse ceremonials of gifts are intrinsic to ethnic cultures whether primitive or more advanced. It is a trait of being "human." As has been observed, in a quote often attributed to Winston Churchill, Britain's famous leader: "We make a living by what we get, but we make a life by what we give." Or more expressively, there is the Chinese folk-saying: "If you want happiness for an hour, take a nap. If you want happiness for a day, go fishing. If you want happiness for a year, inherit a fortune. If you want happiness for a life time, help somebody."[25]

For the Christian, then, we accept that all humanity has been created "in God's image and likeness." Friendship is a basic constituent of this quality of being human. But transcending all human categories of relational human life is God's revelation and experience of his friendship to us, which transforms all categories and experiences of human friendship. Friendship is universal, but Christian love is unique.

---

25. Jenni Santi, *The Giving Way to Happiness,* p. xviii.

6

Maturity and Wisdom in the Seasons of Life

The traditional family or household in Japan was the *Ie* system. This had a variety of meanings: a building for a residence; a family or household; an extended family group; and a family line of ancestral descendants. This system was originally based on the worship of ancestors, who were thought to provide continuance of the family into the future. Patriarchism was a major characteristic; the position of women low and concern for succession a high priority. All this had strong Confucian roots, overlaid by later Buddhist rites. This was codified in 1898 and remained until the American occupation in 1945 when the old civil code was revised.[1] Then the *ie* system was abolished, to give equal rights to men and women, making divorce much easier, as it was now exercised by mutual consent. There was also a dramatic rise of nuclear families over extended families; now, the individual is in ascendance over the *ie* tradition.

Yet seniority rules, called *Sempai-Kohai,* still dominate Japanese society. "Seniors" are called *sempai*, they are usually

---

1. Roger J. Davies, *The Japanese Mind: Understanding Contemporary Japanese Culture* (Tokyo: Tuttle Publishing, 2002), pp. 122-123.

older, but the term could be extended to those with superior intellect. *Kohai* are the "followers," providing symmetry, which American leadership culture has not had, since no reference is given to "the followers." This can explain a great deal of the contemporary political turbulence in American culture, when everything depends on the leader rather than the substance of the society.

Youth culture, too, is stabilized by Japanese *sempai-kohai*. But the break-down of business companies is creating a new erosion of *sempai-kohai,* if executives fail as business leaders, or indeed if pastors fail in their congregations. High recognition everywhere is becoming more functionally given, whereas traditionally it was granted.

Western "Ageism" Versus Japanese Respect for Elders

The demographic aging of Japanese society has become a serious national concern, with its restricted immigration of youth. For modern people are living longer, which exasperates an aging society like Japan. But the problem in Japan profoundly affects the national budget. The psychologist Karl von Dürckheim once asked Japanese scholars what was considered the supreme good of Japan. "Our old people," he was told. Perhaps that may be why the physiological maximum length of human life is 125 years, and there are records of such individuals having lived that long in Japan. There is still a national holiday in Japan to celebrate the aged, called "Honor the Aged Day"!

While Western culture is being much more revitalized demographically, it is experiencing heavy losses of cultural heritage and wisdom, by its prejudice of "ageism." It is a serious loss both for the society as well as within Christian church life.[2] The great potential resource, both in society and in churches, of the wisdom of mature seniors is being discarded wantonly. In turn, feeling worthless, Western seniors often face a crisis of social invisibility, like being "in the outpatient department of Purgatory," before they die.[3] Here Western Christians have so much to learn from Japanese Christian families, where youth still respect their seniors, and are more willing to gain their wisdom of maturity "in Christ." But the whole new professional industry of gerontology has created a flood of books, making the whole field of aging more indeterminate than ever before.[4] Meanwhile, East or West, the impact of technology threatens to de-value the "wisdom of ageing" in place of technical skills, as we discussed in our opening essay.

Wisdom as Reflective of Our Humanity

Universally, wisdom has had similar basic features. It is always knowledge transmitted from parents to their children. Didactic texts of this kind occur in Egypt from 2300 B.C. onwards. Sometimes this is also in a school setting, such as is found in another Egyptian text, *The Instruction of a*

2. James M. Houston and Michael Parker, *The Challenge of the Ageing Church* (Downers Grove, Illinois: Inter-Varsity Press, 2013).

3. There is much literature, but see James M. Houston & Michael Parker, *A Vision for the Aging Church: Renewing Ministry for and by Seniors* (Downer's Grove, Illinois: Inter-Varsity Press, 2011).

4. See *Handbook of Theories of Aging*, ed. Vern L. Bengson et al (New York: Springer Publishing Co.: 2009). It exhibits an industry of statistics and communicates very little!

Man for his Son, vividly describing school education. The Old Testament book of Proverbs, in Prov. 22:17-23:14 seems almost a direct quote of Egyptian instructions of the twelfth or thirteenth century B.C.[5] The earliest text in Mesopotamia for the formal teaching of wisdom is that of a father, Shuppak, to his son, Ziusudra, the hero of the Sumerian flood epic. Later in the eighth century B.C., Ahikar's wise instructions persisted until into Christian times; Proverbs 12:13f. and 27:3 echo his instructions. Canaanite-Phoenician wisdom was also exchanged with the Israelites, and the personified Wisdom of Proverbs 8 may well have originated in the female Phoenician deity, the goddess Queen (*milkat*).[6] Indeed, into the New Testament we find the same use of Greek and Roman parental instructions on wisdom, as in the *Sentences of Sextus*.[7]

Likewise, the merit of proverbs is that they are also timeless, whether from West or East. As the first Spanish novelist, Cervantes, remarked: "proverbs are short sentences drawn on long experiences." To which we can draw the corollary that wisdom comes from reflecting on long experiences. The Japanese perhaps much more than our Western societies today still make wise, wide use of their proverbs. An educational card game for Japanese children, based on *iroha* syllabary, is played with two sets of 48 picture cards each,

---

5. "Wisdom," *The International Standard Bible Encyclopedia* (Grand Rapids, Michigan: William B. Eerdmans Publishing Company, vol. 4, 1988), pp. 1074-5.
6. Ibid, p. 1075.
7. Ibid, p. 1082.

the first syllable introducing a proverb.[8] Two hundred such proverbs are still memorized by Japanese children in child education. Many Japanese proverbs are lost in the folk-lore of antiquity, others are sourced in Chinese, to show the influence of Confucian ethics and of Buddhist teachings. All illustrate a Japanese proverb: "*Ninjo ni kokkyo nashi*," which means, "there are no barriers to human nature."[9] Indeed, in 1940, a Japanese scholar, Hitoshi Mizukami, collected 1,259 maxims and sayings, and translated them into English and Japanese.

The Golden Rule appears in both Japanese/Confucian and Christian languages: "What you do not wish done to you, do not unto others" (cp. Matt. 7:12). "If you put spittle on your eyebrows, the fox will not bewitch you." This refers to the belief of many cultures that spittle has medicinal values, which the incidents of Jesus healing blind men also demonstrates (e.g., Mark 7:33). "All that take up the sword will be destroyed by the sword" (Matt. 26: 52), is a biblical proverb that has been translated into many languages. This universality of wisdom reflects once more the *imago dei*, as the basic constitution of all humanity. Yet to remain there is to assume such wisdom is humanistic—which it is!

Distinctives of Biblical Wisdom

But Biblical wisdom is not humanistic in origin. A search for order, living meaningfully, the quest for authority, the

---

8. David Galef, *Japanese Proverbs, Wit and Wisdom* (Tokyo/New York: Tuttle, 2012).

9. Daniel Crump Buchanan, *Japanese Proverbs and Sayings* (Norman: University of Oklahoma Press, 1965), pp. xv-xvi.

desire to be motivated and inspired, yes, these are human desires. Proverbs, folk tales and sayings, these all respond to these needs. Jesus, too, spoke in parables, as the desire of the crowd to seek wise teaching. But Biblical wisdom originates in God, not in human nature. It teaches uniquely that "the fear of the Lord is the beginning of wisdom" (Prov. 9:10; Gen. 20:10-11; Exod. 1:17; Deut.4:6). This "Lord" is monotheistic, unlike the fear of the gods, while its "fear" is moral not craven fear, personal not impersonal. As "the giving God," he gives us what we could never achieve for ourselves, contrastive to the human "wisdom" which is "masterful understanding," gained by one's own life experiences.

Job is rightly asking, "Where can wisdom be found? Mortals do not comprehend its worth; it cannot be found in the land of the living…it is hidden from the eyes of every living thing" (Job 28:13,21; cp. Prov. 1:7; Eccles.12:13-14). Old age does benefit from accumulating more "wisdom" than youth, but this is not Biblical wisdom, where a child can be wise in the Kingdom of God, and the old can remain as fools. In Biblical wisdom, described by the apostle Paul as "God's secret wisdom," it is only revealed and given by Jesus Christ, himself the Wisdom of God, only revealed to us by the Holy Spirit (1 Cor. 2: 6-16). Echoing the words of Isaiah 64:4, the apostle is also making reference to the three foolish friends of Job, who like Eliphaz did not "see," or Bildad, who did not "hear," or Elihu, whose mind had not conceived, precisely what they claimed were sources of their own "wisdom."

> "No eye has seen,
> no ear has heard,
> no mind has conceived
> what God has prepared for those
> who love him" (1 Cor. 2: 9).

Biblical Role of Elders

It has become common in the West to speak of older people as "seniors." Lost has become the concept of "elders," which the most primitive tribes of Africa, Australia, and Southeast Asia still conserve. Their role is to pass on from generation to generation their culture, with its skills to survive and to benefit the social and spiritual well-being of future generations. Advances in civilizations, ancient and modern, lose this ability in new divisions of labor. Likewise, institutionalized religion(s) do the same thing, with new hierarchies of worship and teaching the faith(s).

But when Christianity originated and began to spread through the Roman empire, eldership was spontaneous. In the church plantings the apostle Paul made, the appointment of elders became a general practice. Paul charges Titus to appoint elders in every town, to nurture and foster the new household of believers (Titus 1:5). Such elders were to be relational, exemplary in his own home life, hospitable, a lover of good, self-controlled, upright, holy and disciplined (Titus 1:6-9). As Paul further teaches: "For if anyone does not know how to manage his own family well, how can he take care of God's church?" (1 Tim. 3:5). The simplicity of eldership is expressive of its essential quality, which nothing else can substitute—no priest, no bishop, no pope.

1. *Elders enlarge our vision*

Having lived much longer than youth, elders are privileged with greater horizons of living. Today, they are seeing rapid cultural changes in their own lifetime. They should have, then, less "tunnel-vision." The maturity of their achievements are the norm. Origen, the first great scholar of textual study of the Scriptures, interpreted Paul's epistles as those of a young man writing to the Corinthian Christians, also young in faith, in contrast to the more mature Roman or Thessalonian Christians, and the most mature Colossian and Ephesian Christians. Thus we can trace how Paul's own vision for the Gospel is constantly growing and being enlarged. Likewise, many times over we can see how a great Christian thinker like Augustine of Hippo is growing with an enlarging vision as he progresses from the *Confessions,* to *The City of God,* to his *Expositions on the Psalms.* Great classics are the works of mature creators, as we see in Dante's *Commedia*, in John Bunyan's *Pilgrim's Progress*, and so many others. William Blake did his finest artistic work, *Illustrations to the Book of Job*, when he was 70.

2. *Elders are devoted to prayer*

The early Fathers of the Church were constantly in prayer for their congregations. More than any other service, they are most constantly asked to intercede in prayer by those who respect them. It is reported that just before his martyrdom, at the long age of 86, Polycarp spent two hours "remembering all who had ever come his way, both small and great, low or high." Much of the composition of Paul's letters are prayers, such as the wonderful prayer of Ephesians 1:18-23.

How blessed are the old members of our churches, who in their wheelchairs or sickly in bed, can only have a daily ministry of prayer. After six years of public life as the bishop of Kronstadt in St. Petersburg, Ilyich Sergiyev devoted the rest of his long life in writing hundreds of letters of counsel and prayer to unknown strangers who wrote him from throughout the Russian empire.[10]

3. Elders live in the face of death

Old people are constantly losing loved ones, often visiting them as they lie dying. These experiences blend life and death in ways younger people do not normally experience. For Christians, then, only a thin membrane separates this life and the life to come. This gives a new depth to their faith, a quality of living as a Christian gained in no other way than being in the constant presence of death.

In contrast, "medicalized death," as physicians constantly experience, trivializes death, for they are engaged in the physicality of dying, not entering into the mysterious threshold between this moral life and eternal life. Nor can they—without a Christian faith—believe in Paul's affirmation that the cross of Christ has destroyed the power of death, in "the death of death by the resurrection of Christ from the dead" (1 Cor. 15:35-58).

The role of Christian elders is then to maintain a strong connection between our baptism of faith and our

---

10. John of Kronstadt, *My Life in Christ*, trans. by E.E. Goulaeff (London: Cassell & Co., 1897).

final mortal death, holding our intermediate life in the tension between these two events. For already our baptism is expressive of spiritual death, in "bearing in our bodies the dying of the Lord Jesus, that the life also of Jesus may be seen in us" (2 Cor 4:10).

Thereby, we distinguish two kinds of resurrection. Firstly, there is a "horizontal resurrection," which passes morally through others, as the apostle decides to share, enjoining all fellow Christians to decide, too, that: "For me to live is Christ, and to die is gain" (Phil. 1:21). It is the exchange of one kind of life for another, now shared together, transmitted in words, acts, and thoughts into those of others.[11] This is a very different outlook from that of the Japanese proverb, "old men are for consultation, while the young are still vigorous to defend self-interest." How contrastive is the Christian life as "transmissive" or "imminent" resurrection!

Secondly, there is a "vertical" or "transcendent resurrection." This reaches back to the memory of God, who the apostle praises, "as the God and Father of our Lord Jesus Christ, who has blessed us in the heavenly realms with every spiritual blessing in Christ. For he chose us in him before the creation of the world to be Holy and blameless in his sight. In love he adopted us to be his sons through Jesus Christ ...." (Eph. 1:3-6). Henceforth our identity is safe, regardless of our aging fear of dementia, for the present life.

---

11. Paul Ricoeur, *Critique and Conviction*, trans. Kathleen Blamey (New York: Columbia University Press, 1998); also Paul Ricoeur, *Living Up to Death,* trans. David Pellauer (Chicago, London: The University of Chicago Press, 2009).

It is a wonderful comfort for Christians to know we live between this life and the life to come.

Likewise, elders attending the dying, with the faith of Christ in their inner being, are like a lighthouse beam of light, standing on the Rock of Ages, in the midst of death, where there is no ultimate death. I experienced that as I held–for 24 hours, a day of days–the slight but steady pressure of my beloved wife's finger intertwined with mine, each knowing the other's presence, both dwelling in the presence of God. For there is found fullness of joy; there all is light and life. For those without Christ, death is more real than life, as they face their mortality. But for those "in Christ," life is infinitely far more real than death. As Xavier Leon-Dufour has said: "it is through death that existence is definitely assured."[12] Such should be the realism of our elders in our Christian communities.

4. Christian elders are a living curriculum of the Christian Life

The aged apostle John praises the youth for their combative strength, but it is not physical strength he is praising but spiritual strength in overcoming evil, indeed "the evil one" (1 Jn. 2:13). But he praises "the fathers," as he calls the elders, "because you have known him that is from the beginning," which he reiterates twice (1 Jn. 2:14).

As we are learning, to reveal one's identity is to reveal a narrative of how I was born, how I lived within a culture,

---

12. X. Leon-Dufour, *Life and Death in the New Testament: the Teachings of Jesus and Paul*, trans. Kathleen Blamey (New York: Columbia University Press, 1998), p. 32f., cp. Mk. 8:35; Lk. 9:24; Lk. 17:33; Matt. 10:39; Jn.12:25.

and how I am still alive within networks of other relationships. A Christian elder's life should be narrated within a church community, to enrich the whole community, as a life well-lived. Each phase of life has its own appropriateness, but like vintage wine, it is best enjoyed most by and through the testimony of "mature Christians." In periods of "Revivals" much focus was given to such "narratives," but in measured balance, space and time for elders to share their stories would be both appropriate and enriching for the whole community. For our Christian faith is expressed in embodiment, culturally and personally so.

7

Enriched by Christian Japanese Insights on Suffering, Silence, and Beauty

Educated Japanese Christians are more familiar with Western theologians and their writings than Western Christians are with Japanese scholars. Yet, as we have seen, Japanese are also more self-aware of their own distinctive cultural anthropology. For they have had to protect themselves from the much older and more powerful nation of China. Being distinctive and yet also being absorbent has been their cultural axis. The latter is called *Itoko-Dori*—endless assimilations of external cultures throughout its history, within its own mind-set.

A recent Japanese work by Atsuyoshi Fujiwara, *Theology of Culture in a Japanese Culture,* continues this tradition theologically. However, instead of continuing the eclecticism and syncretism of absorbing other religions into Japanese, the author is trying to adopt the thoughts of H. Richard Niebuhr (*Christ and Culture*), or Karl Barth, or

Emil Brunner, or, indeed, John Howard Yoder.[1] In contrast, we are seeking to reverse this orientation, to explore what Western Christians can gain and be inspired by through the rich Japanese Christian heritage.

The '*Dō*' Spirit of Ambiguity

A great cultural spell over the Japanese mind is "the *Dō* spirit," a form of pantheism incommunicable by the spoken or written word. It influences both domestic and everyday life, as well as scholarly, aesthetic, dramatic, and philosophical activities.[2] It explains why outsiders use metaphors like "swamplands" to describe its culture. It has led Japan, especially through Zen Buddhism, which originated in Taoism, to teach the essential unity of man and nature. "Teaching without words," it is not grasped but received. Its disciples go through a cathartic process of emptying the mind of all passions and distinctions, to become aware of possessing the Buddha-nature within themselves. Introduced into Japan in the twelfth century, its training is about "the eternal now," without interposing thoughts or ideas.

In Zen, "opposites are relational and so fundamentally harmonious," whether it be light or darkness, trust or betrayal, politeness or indescribable cruelty, stillness or action.[3] For all Zen paradoxes transcend opposites. Such a

---

1. Atsuyoshi Fujiwara, *Theology of Culture in a Japanese Context: A Believers' Church Perspective* (Eugene, Oregon: Pickwick Publications, 2012).

2. Roger J. Davies & Osamu Ikeno, *The Japanese Mind* (Tokyo/New York: Tuttle, 2002), pp. 71-82.

3. A. Watts, *The Way of Zen* (New York: Pantheon, 1957), p. 175.

Japanese mind-set of *Dō* deepens the human condition in the most startling colors. For as well as being the politest and most aesthetic, with quietude, obedience, and respect as its moral qualities, it can also be most brutal, violent, and demonic.[4] Teaching that one should exist deeply inside and be slightly expressive outside, Japanese Zen is contrary to Western education.[5] So, Westernized business leaders from their perspective recognize and condemn *do* as the Achilles heel of Japanese culture. In paradox, Japanese impersonal culture has dramatically advanced robotics, yet at the same time, this is wholly contradicted by the daily domesticity that is given to the trees and the stones and the aesthetics of Japanese landscapes.

The whole modern life of Japan would totally collapse if those who participate in modern city life practiced the Zen way. Yet the Japanese mind-set accommodates both, with the underlying assumption that "opposites are harmonious"! No wonder the culture seems such a forested swampland to the outsider, as sinking into the primordial.[6] Strikingly, the Biblical motif is "the garden," by which Western civilization has been inspired.[7] The only merit is that the Japanese may be less hypocritical than their Western Christians, in probing the guileful deceits of sin, which we all instinctively

---

4. Makoto Fujimura, *Silence and Beauty: Hidden Faith Born of Suffering* (Downers Grove: Inter-Varsity Press, 2016), p. 16-18.

5. A. Pinnington, *Inside Out: English Education and Japanese Culture* (Tokyo: Sansyusha, 1986).

6. Robert Pogue Harrison, *Forests: The Shadow of Civilization* (Chicago: The Chicago University Press, 1992).

7. Robert Pogue Harrison, *Gardens: An Essay on the Human Condition* (Chicago: The Chicago University Press, *2008).*

hide. Certainly, Japanese Christians are far more aware of the evils of idolatry all around them.

"Conversion" as the Beginning and the Onward Pilgrimage

Imagine, then, the fortitude of the first Christian missionaries, from the Portuguese Jesuit Xavier in the 1560s, until modern times, trying to persuade their first Christian converts. Reflect, too, on the courage of the witnesses of Christ, cruelly martyred for their faith during the early seventeenth century! How did the Christian Gospel ever penetrate the Japanese *psyche*? The controversial novel by Endo, *Silence*, illustrates this seventeenth-century cultural confrontation.

Kenzaburo Oe commented in his Nobel speech on this polarization of such deep ambiguity, of the Japanese as both inflictor of terror and also the victim of terror. He titled his speech, "Japan, the Ambiguous, and Myself": "... after 120 years of the opening of the country, present-day Japan is split between two opposite poles of ambiguity. I too am living as a writer with this polarization imprinted on me like a deep scar."[8]

A diary of a Japanese youth of the mid-nineteenth century is revealing. Kanzo Uchimura was the son of a well-educated Confucian scholar, invited one Sunday morning to go with him to:

> ...a certain place in foreigners' quarters, where we can hear pretty women sing, and a big tall man with a long beard shout and howl upon an elevated place, flinging

8. Quoted in Makoto Fujimura, *op. cit.*, p. 72.

> his arms and twisting his body in all fantastic manners, to all which admittance is entirely free… conducted in the language which was new to me then… Christianity was an enjoyable thing to me so long as I was not asked to accept it. Its music, its stories, the kindness shown me by its followers, pleased me immensely. But five years after, when it was formally presented to me to accept it, with certain stringent laws to keep and much sacrifice to make, my whole nature revolted against submitting myself to such a course. That I must set aside one day out of seven specially for religious purpose, wherein I must keep myself from all my other studies and enjoyments, was a sacrifice which I thought next to impossible to make.[9]

Then, too, to betray the gods of the Japanese nation, was to become a traitor to his own people. The subsequent harsh ignorance of the foreign missionaries further compounded his impasse. But finally, aged 16, on June 2, 1877, he was baptized, re-naming himself Jonathan, "because I was a strong advocate of the virtue of friendship, and Jonathan's love of David pleased me well."[10] There follows a long diary of how Kanzo/Jonathan "*became* a Christian," hoping to later write another book on "how I *worked* as a Christian."[11]

A doctoral thesis published in 1915 by Katsuji Kato helps us gain some further insight into the obstacles to Japanese becoming Christians. Gathering the private reports of 35 interviews, together with historical narratives, Kato

9. Kanzo Uchimura, *How I Became a Christian: Out of My Diary* (Memphis: General Books, 20012), p. 3.
10. Ibid, p. 5.
11. Ibid, p. 51.

recorded his insights in the context of Western efforts to understand "the psychology of conversion."[12] He observed several features of Japanese converts.

1. Religious education was more social and communal than religious among middle-class children, unprepared then for Sunday school teaching, as it was first introduced to Japan in the 1890s. Children were emotionally not trained to be devotional; this was new for them. Many early converts were small children before the age of puberty, who contrasted life at home with that of the Sunday school, attended for a "better education."

2. Older, more educated children were receiving a more intellectual Confucian mind-set, for which emotional changes of puberty had no relevance.

Later teenage youth, seeking heroes, found in their Christian teachers more self-recognition, understanding, and encouragement, both in exercise of mind and in bodily sports, than in the Japanese system of education.

3. More intellectual conversions were found among adults, who were able to more fully reflect upon the Gospel of Christ.

4. This often occurred later, in periods of crisis, such as sickness in the family, failure in business, with the appeals of restoration, redemption, and re-assurance. As this progresses, the process of "being converted" becomes "re-generation," with more moral fruitage of new virtues, freedom

---

12. Katsuji Kato, *The Psychology of Oriental Religious Experience: A Study of Some Typical Experiences of Japanese converts to Christianity* (Menasha, Wisconsin: George Banta Publishing Co., 1915).

from old vices, and a markedly qualitative change in outlooks on life.

5. Gradually, there is increasing awareness that the Christian life is becoming more consciously "supernatural." There is increasing awareness of conscious dependence upon God, with less nominal adherence and habitual attitudes. One becomes more decisive and possessed of resolute determination "to be a Christian." No longer is one merely "religious," for now the identity of "being a Christian" is more widely known in the community.

In the life-long process of "becoming a Christian," we interpret eldership as the mark of its maturity, West or East. Such Christian maturity is marked by the intensification of personal growth, of no longer a self-life, but "a self-for-the-other," in both identity and practice. It is profoundly "life in Christ," penetrating and radiating ever more widely into the whole society, secular or religious. Synergies of encounter and co-operation widen in ever greater circles, all clearly "supernatural," because God's presence is visible and effective. Life is now no longer about "I," but all about "we."

Human Suffering and the Suffering God

A powerful way we reach out to "the other," is in the shadowy presence of suffering. Nobel Prize winner Kenzaburo Oe recites his candid story of the birth of his first son, Hikari, who was born with a brain abnormality. He explores in several essays how his family bonds would have grown weaker and weaker, resulting in a cheerless home, with their embrace of Hikari, along with his handicapped life. How much more knowledgeable of being "human," how much more compassionate, how much more mature all had become![13]

All suffering assaults our traditional values, but distinctively in his novels, such as *Hiroshima Notes,* which considers the nuclear attack on Hiroshima, Kenzaburo Oe portrays the political consequence of the Emperor being no longer a god.[14] Japan, then, has suffered culturally the full embrace of natural disasters such as frequent earthquakes, occasional tsunamis, typhoons, as well as terrifying wars, intense family handicaps, and starvation.

But what Japanese Christian Kazoh Kitamori introduced was the unthinkable: "the Suffering God." Just as Martin Luther was enveloped in suffering, human and divine,[15] Kazoh Kitamori has, as a Lutheran, the same focus on suffering, both human and divine, as appropriate to the events of the twentieth century.[16] Inspired by the Old Testament prophets, Kitamori interprets Jeremiah "as a man who saw the heart of God deeply," and who allowed him to also experience the depth of God.[17]

Quoting from 1 Peter 2:24, Kitamori then argues, "God in pain is the God who resolves our human pain by his own. All kinds of *pain experienced in this world remain*

---

13. Kenzaburo Oe, *A Healing Family,* trans. Stephen Snyder (Tokyo/New York, Kodansha International, 1995), p. 95.

14. Kenzaburo Oe, *A Personal Matter,* trans. John Nathan (New York: Grove Press, 1969).

15. Dennis Ngien, *The Suffering of God: According to Martin Luther's "Theologia Crucis"* (Vancouver: Regent College Publishing, 1995), pp. 19-54.

16. Kazoh Kitamori, *Theology of the Pain of God,* trans. Shinkyo Shuppansha (Richmond, Va.: John Knox Press, 1965).

17. Ibid, p. 20.

meaningless and fruitless as long as they do not serve the pain of God. We must take care not to suffer human pain in vain."[18] It is helpful to compare his insights with the Western contribution of Terence E. Fretheim in *The Suffering of God: an Old Testament Perspective,* in which the theme is explored more broadly.[19]

Just as the apostle Paul did not know Christ "after the flesh" (2 Cor. 5:16), yet definitely he knew him "in the flesh" (Rom. 8:3). Likewise, Kitamori linked the pain of God with the historical Jesus, as also the love of God with the sufferings of Jesus on the cross, his teaching with his Person. That is why the whole life of Jesus is profoundly the *via dolorosa.*[20]

Now Kitamori is further challenged by Hebrews 2:10: "For it was *fitting* that he, for whom and by whom all things exist, in bringing many sons to glory, should make the pioneer of their salvation perfect through suffering." For the Greeks it is the impassibility of God that expresses his deity.[21] In contrast, it is the New Testament human/divine suffering of God that reveals his *being,* human and divine. Worshipfully, Kitamori contemplates the cross of Christ, as Paul does in declaring, "I am determined to know nothing among you save Christ and him crucified" (1 Cor. 2:2). For this is the action of the *immanent* Trinity, where divine "generation" as the Father and the Son, are distinguished

---

18. Ibid, p. 21.

19. Terence E. Fretheim, *The Suffering of God: An Old Testament Perspective* (Philadelphia: Fortress Press, 1984).

20. Kazoh Kitamori, Ibid, pp. 32-43.

21. Paul Gavrilyuk, *The Suffering of the Impassible God: The Dialectics of Patristic Thought* (Oxford: Oxford University Press, 2004).

from the divine "procession," as the Son proceeding God the Holy Spirit.[22]

Christian ethics and service follow from these profound Biblical insights of Kitamori. Now he quotes Matthew 16:24: "If any man would come to me," says our Lord Jesus Christ, "let him deny himself and *take up his cross* and follow me." For "he who does not *take up his cross* and follow me is not worthy of me" (Matt. 10: 38). The testing of Abraham on Mount Moriah, to see "if he feared God" (Gen. 22:1,12), is the crucial test of all Christian discipleship, yet its significance Kitamori admitted "has not yet been fully known."[23] But in his conclusion, Kitamori noted that the Hebrew word *hamat* is translated simultaneously as both love and pain![24] "Love rooted in the pain of God" concerns the whole message of the Bible—all that we mean by the Christian Gospel!

A recent Western scholar, apparently unaware of Kitamori's teachings, has amplified the narrative of pain and suffering as endured by the early Christians to become communities of sufferers. Judith Perkins sees the recognition

---

22. Ibid, pp. 44-49.
23. Ibid, pp. 50-51.
24. Kitamori, Ibid, p. 162.

and role of the sufferer as one's Christian identity, and as "essential for the growth of Christianity as any institution."[25]

Silence, as Deeper, Truer Communication

When the friends of Job first witnessed his sufferings, they were appropriately in silence for seven days. "No one said a word to him, because they saw how great was his suffering" (Job 2:13). Only when they all began to talk was there discord and distrust, for the next 35 chapters, until the Lord silences them all with his final speech.

In their concept of *Chinmoku,* Japanese culture has much to teach our more vocal communication in the West, with the truthfulness of silent communication. Yes, "silence" can mean saying nothing, or else communicating everything! Associated with *Haragei,* it means implicit mutual understanding, and with *Ishin denshin,* intuitive telepathy. For long in their history, Japanese have valued silence as a form of truthfulness, located not in the lungs but in the belly, just as the Hebrews located truth in the organ of the heart. As the anthropologist S. Lebra explains: "Components of the outer self, such as face, mouth, spoken words, are in contrast [i.e. to the belly] associated with cognitive and moral falsity. Truthfulness, sincerity, straight-forwardness, or reliability

---

25. Judith Perkins, *The Suffering Self: Pain and Narrative Representation in the Early Christian Era* (London/New York: Routledge, 1995), p. 214.

are allied to reticence. Thus a man of few words is trusted more than a man of many words."[26]

Zen Buddhism has again had a great influence on this emphasis upon silence. For the goal of Zen is being implicit, not explicit; appealing to the intuitive, not to the cognitive, role of the mind. This requires a constant practice of quietude, contemplation, and self-emptying, before an external realm of emptiness and silence.[27]

That is why in traditional Japanese music, silent intervals called *Ma*, are central while sounds play an auxiliary role in marking *ma*. Likewise, in *Kabuki* dramas and *Noh* plays the silence between the lines expresses excitement, tension, and climax. All Japanese arts are rooted in this primary need of empty space or silence.

Another reason for silence is group consciousness. The saying, "The nail that sticks out will be hammered in," emphasizes that to insist upon one's own opinion, or to show off, or appear to be an egotist, are all signs of being thoughtless of others, impolite, immature, and worse! One has to learn to know one's place in a hierarchy of social consciousness, within the whole group present, or within the whole society itself. We all assume that when one is silent, one may have nothing to "say," and yet have something to "think." It requires a right relationship for us in the West to have the courage or conviction to speak the truth.

"Reserve and restraint" (*enryo-sasshi*) we all have; some more than others! Some are more sensitive than others! At

26. S. Lebra, "The Cultural Significance of Silence in Japanese Communication," *Multilingua*, 6, 1987, p. 345.
27. Roger J. Davis, & Osamu Ikeno, ed. *The Japanese Mind* (Tokyo: Tuttle Publishing, 2001), p. 52.

the same time, we all can be irritated if a close friend or family member does not communicate adequately what they are privately keeping in their silence. The pace of urban life is much faster than in rural environments, so the urbanite "does not have time," nor the personality, to interpret the wide range of meanings for silence, such as sympathy, modesty, agreement, patience, and even negatives such as embarrassment, resentment, lack of forgiveness, defiance, apathy, and pride.[28]

As a young earnest Christian I failed to integrate the two worlds I was living in. As the Bursar of my Oxford college, I needed to linger over the college evening dinner, to be part of the collegial life. But every Tuesday evening I rushed out early, to travel to the church prayer meeting, where I, as an elder, was always late! Failure in verbalization resulted in both positions and places! Appropriate silence and absence would have relieved a lot of tension.

Deeper than words, the Christian mystics have experienced the contemplative life. The sevenfold stages of the prayer life of Teresa of Avila, or the degrees of entry into the sufferings of Christ that Julian of Norwich participated with her Lord, can be more readily appreciated by Japanese Christians. Yet for all lovers, words are not needed, and contemplative prayer is for all Christians richer than verbal expressions of prayer. However, if few verbal prayers are made in a Western church prayer-meeting, it is judged as not very "successful." Whereas in a Japanese prayer meeting silence can be accepted as more enriching of the soul.

---

28. Takie Lebra, *Identity, Gender, and Status in Japan,* 1987, pp. 116-121.

Strange, then, that the Quaker movement has never been successful in Japan!

The Aesthetic in the Context of Silence

An inspiring Christian Japanese artist who uses his handicapped life creatively is Tomihiro Hoshino (b. 1946). He composes poems and paintings with a brush in his mouth because he was totally paralysed below his neck, by a terrible accident while coaching a gymnastic club. He wanted to communicate with his wife, so he began to use words sparingly like jewels of thought in simple poems. He then began to paint to fill the empty space on the paper with a single flower, because he could only see what was directly in front of him. At first, his characters as words and his paintings were blurred, needing his wife's gentle hand to sharpen their profiles.

Two years later, he became a Christian, now seeing the beauty of God's creation in very small things: a cicada, a butterfly, a bell-flower, a walnut on a twig. All these he sees in his lovely book, *In the Palms of Your Hand*. He concludes by confessing:

> There are many things I can't do, since I lost use of my hands and feet. On the other hand, there are things I became able to do. One of them is to write poems... for me words are equal to walking and moving fingers. How I use them makes my everyday life like heaven or like hell. The words added to my paintings are born

out of such a life...if we know we are imperfect, it is natural to help each other.[29]

29. Tomihiro Hoshino, *In the Palm of Your Hands,* trans. Yoshiaki and Fumiko Yui (Tokyo: Kaisei-sha Publishing Co., 1999), pp. 93-95.

Conclusion

These essays are also incomplete, since the theme of Japanese-Western Christianity is ongoing and indeed inexhaustible. Our plea is for a more authentic Japanese Christianity in an age of massive homogenization. As Uchimura Kanzo has stated: "When a Japanese truly and independently believes in Christ, he is a Japanese Christian, and his Christianity is Japanese Christianity. It is all very simple."[1] Yes, but behind the identity of being "a Christian" lurks a denominational identity—Anglican, Baptist, Catholic, Presbyterian, Orthodox, etc. These are becoming increasingly historical relics in the West, but become even more idiosyncratic in the East. For in the East, the embraced denominations have no relevance to their history or culture. Whereas as we have seen, the apostle Paul remained a Jewish Christian all his life, and urged his mixed ethnic communities to remain within their ethnicity also.

What disrupts the Body of Christ is whenever new charismatic leaders create new movements, which claim to be "more Christian" than the traditional denominations, as evidenced by their new popularity. Here we can be warned by such new Japanese movements as *Makuya* Christianity, which rejected all institutionalized forms of Christianity, to create the absolute individualism and group autonomy

---

1. Uchimura Kanzo, *Sources of Japanese tradition*, ed. Ryusaku Tsunoda, Wm. Theodore de Bary & Donald Keene (New York: Columbia University Press, 1958), vol. 2, pp. 348-50.

of the *Mukyokai*.² This then is no different from the many American movements that, with greater financial resources, have created, and still are creating, ever new movements. Like the Tower of Babel, they are forever generating confusion and discord.³

Again the simple need is for all Christians to have a basic identity of being "in Christ." This should transcend our professional identities, our ethnic identities, even our familial identities. It uniquely claims a supernatural identity, claimed by no other religious faith. "In Christ," then, we bear our suffering, we live in our daily dying unto the Lord Jesus, we communicate our silence, and we express our beauty. Yet we make all these claims in utmost humility, for they are claimed in the name of God the Son, who became human as a man, by the love of God the Father, through the fellowship of God the Holy Spirit, Amen.

---

2. Carlo Caldarola, *Christianity: The Japanese Way* (Leiden: E.J. Brill, 1979).

3. See the broad sweep by Byron Earhart, *Religion in the Japanese Experience: Sources and Interpretations* (Belmont, Ca.: Wadsworth, 2nd ed., 1997).

CPSIA information can be obtained
at www.ICGtesting.com
Printed in the USA
LVOW08s0817200617
538667LV00003B/3/P